Italian cookbook

The Secrets of Italian Cuisine With Authentic and Original Recipes

MARTA CERINA

Ciao! Food is Italy, and Italy is food!

Have you always been a *foodie* who has a tangible passion for authentic and classic Italian cooking? Then this book is for you.

It will take you on a culinary journey through the 20 regions of Italy, with a 'stopover' in each region, where you will find dishes akin to the area.

The recipes are easy to follow and understand. It comes complete with wine pairing suggestions and even a few Italian terms to learn and enjoy.

Embrace your inner Italian and explore all this comprehensive book offers with beautiful images scattered throughout the cookbook.

The recipes that you will find in here provide all the ingredients as well as easy to follow step-by-step instructions on how to achieve perfection!

If you like the book, don't hesitate to tell me your opinion, it is very important to me, I wish you a good reading!

TABLE OF CONTENTS

COOKERY

COOKERY

parkinn.com

Introduction:
Iconic Italian Genealogy

Ciao tutti! Italian heritage is one of the most culture-rich civilizations to date, from its deep roots in the diverse blend of epochal societies such as the Romans and the Samnites, straight through to embracing non-native peoples such as the Greeks and Phoenicians.

Proudly dubbed the birthplace of opera, Italy has many offerings to afford her natives and any visitors. She is famous for cultural components such as:

- Amazing food
- Music
- Renaissance art
- Style

The layout of this beautiful country is intricately shaped to resemble a boot and boasts several world-renowned cities. This country is probably the most famous for its cuisine and its proud people.

The 20 Regions of Italy

Italy is subdivided into 20 different regions, resembling states or provinces—as they are called in other countries. With so many unique characteristics, it can be hard for a first-time traveler to fit in all of the fantastic activities and sights on offer unless you plan to take a trip and just explore Italy on its own.

There are 20 regions in total, of which five are autonomous. Autonomous means that they have a broader sense of freedom in terms of finances, politics, etc. The word autonomy, in itself, means to have a sense of self-governance.

The Five Autonomous Regions of Italy

Friuli-Venezia Giulia

This is one of the smaller regions, located on the northeast side of the country. Don't be fooled by its size, as it offers both dazzling seaside views and mountains that border the Alps. If you fancy yourself both sea and hills during your vacation, then this is, without a doubt, one of the regions to visit on your Italian bucket list.

Fact: According to popular folklore, Friuli was once home to a covenant of wizards, sorcerers, and magicians that performed rituals and other magic such as exorcisms circa the 16th and 17th centuries.

These druids and spellcasters reportedly practiced both good and bad magic, and were summoned to court and sentenced for dabbling in enchantments.

Traditional Food: *Paparot, Strucchi, Tiramisu.*

Sardinia

Planning a trip outside of July and August will afford each visitor the tranquil beach settings that this region offers. On the flip side of the coin, this is an excellent spot for a bit of clubbing and other nocturnal social activities.

Fact: It is said that people from Sardinia have the longest life expectancy in the world. Inhabitants are known to reach considerable centenary numbers in age, with 22 people out of every 100 000 inhabitants. It makes you wonder what their secret is. Is there a mystery that is hidden from the rest of the world?

Traditional Food: *Zuppa Gallurese, Bottarga, Seadas*

Sicily

Sicily is the largest region in Italy and also possesses bragging rights when it comes to the region with the best ancient ruins in the whole of Italy. Challenge yourself and plan a climbing expedition to Mount Etna, which is the biggest active volcano on the European continent.

Fact: Due to the charm and beauty that this region has to present, it is no wonder that it became a preferred filming location for several well-known movies centered around the *Mob Italiano*! The most famous of these has to be *The Godfather Trilogy*, which was filmed in 1972, 1974, and 1990 by none other than Francis Ford Coppola.

Traditional Food: *Arancini, Caponata, Raw Red Prawns*

Trentino-Alto Adige

How about combining a bit of German and Italian at the same time, while only visiting one country? Yes, this is indeed possible! This region formed part of Austria-Hungary since it came into existence and was only seized by Italy in 1919. Interestingly enough, the majority of its people speak German, as opposed to Italian.

Fact: This region is laden with wall upon wall of jagged dolomite. The Dolomite mountain ranges were added to the UNESCO World Natural Heritage list in 2009. The basis of the addition to this exclusive club is attributed to the fact that the formation of this type of limestone started around 250 million years ago as a coral reef underneath the Tethys Ocean.

Traditional Food: *Kaiserschmarren, Canederli, Schiacciatina*

Val D'Aosta

This region is located in Northwest Italy and borders Switzerland and France. It has not one but two medieval castles, making it one of the wealthiest areas in all of Italy. The Courmayeur resort on Mont Blanc that is situated in the Aosta Valley is one of the most fabulous resorts in Europe, frequented as the playground of the rich and famous.

Fact: Although the smallest region in Italy, it boasts a wide range of cultural games and sports. One such example is that of *Fiolet*. *Fiolet* can be practiced both as a team or as an individual sport. The aim of the sport is to bounce an oval-shaped ball resembling an egg (fiolet) off a smooth stone with a wooden mallet. The game is won by the person that hits it the furthest while it is still suspended in the air.

Traditional Food: *Polenta Concia, Vapelenentse Soup, Valdostana Ribs*

The Other 15 Regions of Italy

Abruzzo

Due to the rural location of this scenic region, it is not visited often. Apart from the quaint landscapes, it creates the perfect balance year round, with sunny beaches in summer and crisp, white mountains blanketed with snow in the winter. Many visitors are disheartened to visit this region, due to its poverty-stricken status. It had made a remarkable recovery but suffered a catastrophic blow in 2009 when its capital, L'Aquila, was hit by a massive earthquake.

Fact: It is one of the least population-dense regions in Italy and ranked seventh on the list of Italian regions when it comes to a citizen headcount. There is another significant advantage to this region for oenophiles (wine lovers), Abruzzo has a free red wine fountain. Yes, you can travel and stop for a glass of quality Italian wine on your journey! What about this does not sound great? Right?

Traditional Food: *Pizzelle, Fiadoni, Imballo Abruzzese*

Apulia (Puglia)

The best time of year to visit this tourist-popular region is spring or autumn, as the high summer temperatures might be unbearable to some travelers. Puglia is located in the heel of the Italian boot, as seen on a world map.

Fact: The name Puglia is pronounced as *poo-li-ya* and it is responsible for producing 40% of the country's olive oil demand.

Traditional Food: *Fave e Cicoria, Rustico, Panzerotti*

Basilicata

The region of Basilicata has one of the shortest coastlines in Italy and is located on the instep of the famous boot. It is nestled between Calabria and Puglia and its capital is Potenza. One of its greatest tourist attractions has to be the Neolithic cave dwellings in Matera—which are also a World Heritage Site.

Fact: This region is sometimes overlooked, but a lesser-known fact is that it has a special cultivar of wine called *Aglianicodel Vulture.* This wine has been awarded the highest appellation by the *Denominazione di origine controllata e garantita* (DOCG). This is the highest tier of wine that can be achieved in the Italian wine classification order.

Traditional Food: *Basilicata, Matera Bread, Rafanata*

Calabria

This region forms part of the toe of the Italian *stivale*, with its capital being Catanzaro. Calabria is excellent for a remote hideaway, focused on hiking in the splendor of her four mountain ranges.

Fact: During events and special occasions, the *Calabria*

Tarantella is played, and pairs of men and women dressed in brightly colored costumes of red, green, and white (yes, to honor the Italian flag) feverishly dance to this upbeat and well-known tune. Traditionally, the Tarantella was assumed to be a cure for a tarantula spider bite. It was believed that you could cure yourself of the poison injected by the spider's venom by sweating it out. Today, it is used as a form of seduction when luring a partner... much like some arachnids.

Traditional Food: *Zuppuli, Ginetti, Tartufo*

Campania

Campania is one of the culturally rich regions of Italy. It is densely populated and has five provinces in its confines. The biggest draw to tourists when it comes to this region is the Amalfi Coast. The Greek ruins of Paestum is also a must-see for any archaeological enthusiast.

Fact: The inspiration behind the 1812 ballet *Il Noce di Benevento* is based on an old Italian myth of Benevento's witches from the same region. The tale says that Beneveto became a place of gathering for hexes to meet under a walnut tree. During the day, they disguised themselves and walked among the people, but at night they would confer and chant a terribly evil spell reported to cause horrific events such as miscarriages and abortions to those they cursed.

Traditional Food: *Parmigiana Melanzane, Polpette, Fritto Misto di Mare*

Emilia-Romagna

There are so many wonderful reasons to visit this opulent region, from the F1 motor racing event at the Imola circuit, to the multitude of castles, and not to mention the flavorsome

Modena balsamic vinegar and Parmigiano-Reggiano cheese. If, for no other reason, visit it for the culinary experiences you can indulge in.

Fact: Emilia-Romagna is home to some of Italy's most famed car manufacturers. The list comprises names such as Ferrari, Maserati, and Lamborghini. Be still my beating heart!

Traditional Food: *Borgotaro malfatti, Bolognese Ragú, Erbazzone*

Lazio

This is the third most population dense region in Italy and is home to Rome! With so many historical sites to visit, such as the Vatican, Gaeta, Anzio, Tivoli, Ostia, and Palatine hills, you definitely won't be disappointed if this is your thing. If you fancy yourself a bit of a botanist, you can also visit a Renaissance garden or two.

Fact: Nearly €700 000 coins are tossed into the Trevi Fountain annually. The money is then donated to Caritas to help the poor.

Traditional Food: *Carciofi alla Romana, Quinto Quarto, Puntarelle alla Romana*

Liguria

When visiting this region, you can expect to encounter other exciting sites such as Monaco, Cannes, and San Marino along the way. This region was also home to the famous seafarer Christopher Colombus.

Fact: This region is also known as the Italian Riviera. One of Italy's most famous sauces, pesto, calls Liguria its birthplace.

Traditional Food: *Burrida, Pandolce, Trofie*

Lombardy

Lombardy can brag with a capital that is the home of Italian fashion and extravagant nightlife. This is none other than Milan. One of the other big crowd-pullers that attracts tourists to this region is the expanse of lakes Como and Garda.

The Autodromo Nazionale Monza is also located in this incredible region. It is home to many an Italian Formula 1 race. Native Italian-American son, Mario Andretti, clinched the F1 Driver's World Championship at this very circuit in 1977.

Fact: Happy hour in Milan is an indulgent occurrence, with patrons consuming bitter *aperitivos*, that are mixed into cocktails such as Campari and Negroni. Drink o'clock in this region is simply *la dolce vita*!

Traditional Food: *Cotoletta alla Milanese, Pumpkin Tortelli, Panettone*

Marche

This hidden region produces many of Italy's furniture and textiles. Tourists who have visited this region, prefer it for the quiet, sandy beaches and the R and R that accompanies it.

Fact: Marche has been the official shoe-producing capital of Italy since the 1960s. It is split into three shoe-making repositories that see each repo making a different specialized shoe type. Being Italian and all, there even a Footwear Museum to visit.

Traditional Food: *Moscioli, Olive all'ascolana, Ciausculo*

Molise

This is the newest addition to the list of regions in Italy and is small in scale. Primarily this region is a cultivator of a range of agricultural products such as wine and cereals.

Fact: Molise produces meat and is therefore ideal to visit, if you are looking at experiencing lip-smackingly good Italian food such as *pampanella* and *pezzata*.

Traditional Food: *Composta Molisana, Caciocavallo di Agnone, Cauciuni*

Piedmont

Another item on the Italian to-visit list for foodies! With its slow food organization—meaning the promotion of local food and authentic cooking—you can expect classical Italian dishes from breakfast to dinner.

Fact: Approximately 170 000 acres of the Piedmont region is made up of vineyards. Therefore it comes as no surprise that this region is renowned for some esteemed Italian wine labels.

Traditional Food: *Agnolotti del Plin, Bagna Cauda (also Bagna Caôda), Carne Cruda all'albese*

Tuscany

The Italian Renaissance period is said to have originated in Tuscany as is the Italian language as we know it today. Due to its reputation, this region can be perceived as somewhat mainstream and can be overcrowded at the best of times. Not to mention that it is quite pricey.

Fact: Tuscany was the first European region to adopt sidewalks or pavements as they are more commonly known. The city of Florence became a pioneer of this occurrence in 1339, and soon the rest of Europe followed suit.

Traditional Food: *Torta di Ceci, Aquacotta, Lampredotto*

Umbria

This region is found in the center of the Italian boot. It is the neighboring region of Tuscany and thus is regularly compared to its counterpart.

Fact: A fact that will excite tourists is that underneath the city, a network of tunnels and grottos can be found and explored. During World War II, this tunneling system served as a bomb shelter to its occupants.

Traditional Food: *Lumachine alle Schegginese, Brustengolo, Porchetta*

Veneto

The region of Veneto is very well known across the world for its capital city, Venice. It is one of the Italian regions that boasts the largest number of tourists per year (in excess of 60 million). The intricate canal system, carnivals, and gothic architecture make this a unique part of Italy.

Fact: There are only 400 licensed gondolas in the Venetian fleet, and to become a gondolier is harder than it appears on the surface. Lengthy onboarding and training sessions have to be passed, as well as a history test of Venice, before a gondoliere is issued with a license to drive...or is it steer?

Traditional Food: *Risi e Bisi, Polenta e Uccelli, Pastissada de Caval*

Agriculture, Livestock, Fisheries, Forestry, and More

Agriculture

Italy has subdivided its agriculture into four categories, namely:

- ∉ Field crops
- ∉ Forestry
- ∉ Pastures
- ∉ Tree crops

This country is a crucial rice exporter. Both rice and corn are primarily grown on the Po plain. Second to rice, tomatoes are the next major component produced for exportation, with Naples and Emilia-Romagna yielding the most prominent crops.

Livestock

It is estimated that 10 749 000 acres in Italy consist of pasture and meadows. Inadequate national production forced Italy to import substantial amounts of corn. According to researchers, animal husbandry in 2001 yielded 4 141 000 tons of meat that year (Animal husbandry - Italy - import, farming, n.d.). The production was a culmination of hogs, cattle, sheep, and goats.

Even though Italy has a good production rate, the dairy market is still much underdeveloped today.

Fisheries

In the last four decades of the 20th century, the fish production in Italy increased to almost double. However, the 21st century saw exactly the opposite happen. Between 1998 and 2010, wild fish species were mainly caught in the Mediterranean.

The birth of the aquaculture concept, where species such as algae, aquatic plants, mollusks, fish, and crustaceans from both fresh and saltwater environments are cultivated together and regulated by a controlled environment, has had a notable impact on the fishing sector.

Forestry

Forestry in Italy is primarily made up of trees with broad leaves, whereby conifers, in particular, make up a fifth of the numbers in total. The conifer fauna is predominantly found at the Alpine foothills in Trentino-Alto Adige.

Unfortunately, due to the forests' overutilization by the Romans and other civilizations in the 19th century, there is not much woodland left in Italy. This is mainly due to the wood being used to create items such as mine shafts and railway sleepers, amongst others.

Hunting

Hunting is an all-year activity in Italy. Italy boasts some very well-known gun manufacturers such as Beretta, making its community one that is passionate about hunting game.

Avid hunters can choose between walk-up wing shooting of fowl such as partridges and quail to a driven shoot, stalking wild boar and deer. Hunting is reserved for the picturesque Italian countryside in the Sardinia, Tuscany, and Umbria regions.

The practice is strictly regulated with permits, quotas, and designated hunting areas to ensure year-round controlled activity.

How Italian Food Took the World by Storm

Some readers will be surprised to know that almost 30 years ago, Italian food was considered food for the peasants. There were no Italian chef sensations and no fancy toppings and gelato to have for dessert.

It was still very much loved, even back then. Patrons fondly classified it as pizza with sauces. Since then, Italian food and Mediterranean food, in general, have revolutionized and emerged as gastronomic excellence. Today it is classed as one of the healthiest lifestyles to adapt, with its plethora of authentic classical dishes on offer and culture-centric lifestyles.

The 80s saw chefs making use of and working for the fresh, wholesome ingredients that have become a given in today's modern Italian kitchens. Back then, they did not have access to truffles, prosciutto, or even extra-virgin olive oil. Everything we know about Italian cooking had to be improvised in the earlier years.

Known for its cultural diversity, thanks to a wide variety of different influences over the year by various civilizations, many Italian dishes are simplistic in nature with high flavor profiles.

Italian cooking is centered around the quality of the ingredients being used in the dish instead of swanky cooking methods.

The Italian Kitchen Icon: aka Nonna!

The matriarch of any Italian *famiglia* is lady *nonna*! Who is lady nonna, you may ask? It is none other than the straight-arrow and soft-faced grandma. Unlike many other languages, in the Italian lexicon, the word nonna stays as is. There are no abbreviations and no other pet names used in the traditional sense of the word. *La nonna* is the one that you turn to when you feel like a treat; she is the stalwart and the go-to feminine role model that will pass her secret recipes on to you— well, if you ask nicely, that is.

She radiates love, care, and understanding. She is loud, and she is proud! But make no mistake! Nonna is no pushover, and as much as she loves you, she will put you back on the straight and narrow when you bend your nose out of line. *Un saluto alla vostra nonna!* (Greetings to your grandmother!)

Products of Genuine Italian Origin

Italians are proud custodians of the authenticity and quality associated with their produce. This ensures that they stand out above illicit and counterfeit products inferior in nature that are being passed off as genuine to the public.

Italy has the largest selection of these products on the entire European continent. These products are shielded for their authenticity, classic taste, and components that make them unique and that are native to their region of origin.

The region, or area of origin, refers to the geographic location (in one of Italy's 20 regions) where the product was cultivated by the environmental factors that played a role in the creation thereof, such as water, soil, climate, etc.

Other influences that lend these products their "certificate of excellence" stamp of approval are the culturally affluent history and the covert cooking methods that have made them a success.

Any consumer that invests in the DOP and IGP labeled products has chosen quality.

Unpacking the various labels of authenticity:

Indicazione Geografica Protetta (I.G.P.)

Also known as the Protected Geographical Indication (P.G.I.). This is reserved for products unique to the 20 regions. This seal provides a sense of surety to the consumer when it comes to both quality and authenticity.

Denominazione di Origine Protetta (D.O.P.)

Otherwise known as Protected Designation of Origin (P.D.O.). Similar to its I.G.P. counterpart, this seal represents genuineness and a quality product produced in one of the 20 regions of Italy. The difference between I.G.P. and D.O.P. is that with D.O.P., every detail in the production process is unique to the region of origin, from the cradle to the grave.

In the case of I.G.P., the minimum requirement is for at least one process to be unique to the area of origin.

Specialità Tradizionale Garantita (S.T.G.)

Translated in English as Traditional Specialty Guaranteed (T.S.G.). This label indicates that this particular product (authentic dish or agricultural product) has a set of original features that distinguishes it from other products in the same category.

Some of these features include being made from traditional ingredients or made using traditional cooking processes. It does not have to be mapped to a specific Italian region, as long as the other two conditions mentioned above have been met.

The Essential Pantry Staples for Italian Cooking

With this list of ingredients, you can stock your pantry with the must-have ingredients when cooking Italian food. It can also serve a dual purpose, in that this can form part of your Italian shopping list:

- 00 flour
- All-purpose flour
- Almond flour
- Arborio rice
- A selection of bell peppers
- A selection of dried pasta (Spaghetti, pasta *corta*)
- Balsamic vinegar
- Basil
- Breadcrumbs
- Black peppercorns (freshly ground)
- Canned beans
- Canned tomatoes (peeled, San Marzano is the best)
- Capers
- Carrots

- Celery
- Chicken broth
- Cheeses
- Coffee
- Dried oregano
- Extra virgin olive oil
- Garlic
- Lemon juice
- Italian spices and seasoning
- Nutella or homemade *gianduja*
- Olives
- Onions
- Parmesan cheese
- Polenta
- Porcini mushrooms
- Salt-packed anchovies
- Selection of salamis, sausages, and meats
- Tomato passata (puree)
- Tomato paste
- Truffle oil
- Tuna in olive oil
- White wine vinegar

Wine (for cooking and drinking, of course)

Chapter 1:
Perfect Antipasti

Italians are pioneers when it comes to food. Not only is the food healthier, but describing a typical Italian scene, one finds animated chatter, loud conversations, and people eating slowly, savoring every last morsel on their plates.

Before delving into antipasti, there is one important factor to mention, and that is the correct pronunciation of the word. No one wants to walk around with a scarlet-lettered T for tourist!

Antipasti is deemed the starter, and you will find these typical platters on the table, served as a first course during a traditional Italian family dinner.

Customarily these jaw-droppingly colorful platters serve the purpose of setting the stage for the feast that is about to start. A primary component of these platters is the selection of different hams prevalent.

The Italian Ham Selection

Culatello: This ham originated from the Emilia-Romagna region. It is similar to prosciutto, except that this is made from the meat on the hind leg.

Pancetta: This ham is made from the same cut as bacon but is salted and air-cured instead.

Prosciutto: A dry-cured ham that is served by slicing it thinly before adding it to the platter. It can be subdivided in:

- Crudo di Cuneo, *PDO*, (Piedmont)
- Prosciutto Amatriciano, *PGI*, (Lazio)
- Prosciutto di Carpegna, *PDO*, (Marche)
- Prosciutto di Modena, *PDO*, (Emilia-Romagna)
- Prosciutto di Norcia, *PGI*, (Umbria)
- Prosciutto di Parma, *PDO*, (Emilia-Romagna)
- Prosciutto di San Daniele, *PDO*, (Friuli-Venezia Giulia)
- Prosciutto di Sauris, *PGI*, (Friuli-Venezia Giulia)
- Prosciutto Toscano, *PDO*, (Tuscany)
- Prosciutto Veneto Berico-Euganeo, *PDO*, (Veneto)

Speck: a dry-cured meat similar to that of prosciutto, as it is also made from the hind legs, but in this instance, the difference is that Speck is smoked and also has a more robust flavor in comparison to prosciutto. It has earned the label of P.G.I.

Guanciale: This meat is very fatty on the palate and is made from the cheeks of the pigs. Guanciale is dried for a period of three months to get the best out of the flavor.

Coppa: Part of the salami family and is air-cured. The meat is taken from the shoulder or the neck of the pig.

Antipasti Recipes You Can Try at Home

Taralli Le Puglia

Region of Origin: Apulia (Puglia)

Wine Pairing: Rivera Bombino Bianco

Time: 1 hour, 30 minutes

Serving Size: sufficient for 8 persons

Prep Time: 25 minutes

Cooking Time: 65 minutes

Ingredients:

- 19 oz all-purpose flour
- Extra flour for kneading
- 2 teaspoons sea salt
- 1/4 cup extra-virgin olive oil
- ⅔ cup dry white wine
- Baking sheet lined with parchment paper

Directions:

1. Add flour and sea salt to a bowl. Gradually add the oil while stirring well. Repeat the process with the white

wine.

2. Transfer the dough to a lightly floured surface and knead for at least 10 minutes. Do this until you have achieved a smooth dough with a springy consistency.

3. Preheat the oven to 374°F.

4. Cut the dough into pieces as large as an olive. Roll it in a rope, about ½ cm in thickness. Join the ends together, and firmly press together. Set aside. Repeat the process until all the dough has been rolled and formed.

5. Bring a pot of water to a boil and divide the taralli into small batches. Cook all the taralli in the water until they float to the surface.

6. Transfer them to a plate lined with kitchen towels to drain. Once they are drained, arrange them on the waiting baking sheets.

7. Bake them for 40 minutes until golden brown. Remove from the oven and allow to cool.

Parma Ham Pockets With Asparagus and Peas

Region of Origin: Emilia-Romagna

Wine Pairing: Prosecco, Malvasia, Sauvignon Blanc, Pinot Grigio, Lambrusco

Time: 25 minutes

Serving Size: 12 portions

Prep Time: 25 minutes

Ingredients:

- 2 oz asparagus
- 2 oz fresh peas, shelled
- 4.5 oz squacquerone cheese
- 4.5 oz ricotta
- 1 oz grated pecorino cheese
- 12 slices Parma ham

Directions:

1. Start by washing the asparagus in warm water. Using a potato peeler, cut 12 ribbons, and set aside.
2. Add the peas and remaining asparagus into a pot of boiling water, and blanch for five minutes. Remove from the stove and allow to cool.
3. Finely chop the blanched peas and asparagus with a sharp paring knife.
4. Add the ricotta, squacquerone, and the pecorino into a separate bowl and gently fold together until a stiff consistency has been achieved.
5. Combine the peas and the asparagus into the cheese, and mix until thoroughly combined.
6. Open the ham and place it on a flat surface—spoon 1 serving of the mixture in the middle of the ham.
7. Gather each piece of Parma ham up, and twist it into a pocket/parcel.
8. Tie the elongated top part with a piece of asparagus ribbon. Plate and serve.

Pepperoni all'Acciuga

Meaning: Pepperoni with Anchovy

Region of Origin: Piedmont

Wine Pairing: Syrah, Nero'd Avola

Time: 60 minutes

Serving Size: 6 portions

Prep Time: 10 minutes

Cooking Time: 50 minutes

Ingredients:

- 2 cups red bell peppers
- 2 cups yellow bell peppers
- 2 oz fresh parsley
- 24 anchovy fillets
- 1 garlic clove, peeled
- 2 tablespoons capers
- 2 oz stale bread - crusts removed
- 1 tablespoon white wine vinegar
- 5 oz extra-virgin olive oil
- Sea salt to taste
- Pepper to taste

Directions:

1. Preheat the oven to 392°F.
2. Poke the whole peppers with a fork multiple times, wrap in tin foil. Place them directly on the oven rack. Roast for 45 minutes, turning regularly until they are tender. Remove when done and allow to cool, still in the tinfoil.
3. Prep the salsa verde while you are waiting for the peppers, by adding the anchovies, bread, garlic,

parsley, and vinegar into a food processor. Blitz continuously, adding the oil in intervals. Season to taste. Continue to blitz until a smooth and creamy consistency has been reached.

4. Remove the tinfoil from the peppers, and cut in half. Remove the seeds and the stems. Arrange the peppers on a platter, add spoonfuls of the mixture on top, and garnish them by scattering anchovy fillets on top.

Fregola Salad

Region of Origin: Sardinia

Wine Pairing: Chardonnay, Sauvignon Blanc

Time: 19 minutes

Serving Size: 4 portions

Prep Time: 10 minutes

Cooking Time: 9 minutes

Ingredients:

- 6 oz fregola
- 7 tablespoons olive oil
- 5 oz green olives, pitted and halved
- 1 garlic clove peeled and chopped finely
- 1 tablespoon marjoram
- 10 mint leaves, shredded
- 1 large fresh orange, zested
- 3 tablespoons balsamic vinegar

∉ Sea salt and pepper (optional)

Directions:

1. Bring salted water in a large skillet to a boil on the stove. Add the fregola to the water and cook for 9 minutes. Remove from the heat and drain the water.
2. Toss with 3 tablespoons of the olive oil. Transfer to a large, flat pan and allow to cool completely.
3. While the fregola is cooling down, add the olives, garlic, mint, marjoram, orange zest, remaining olive oil, and vinegar in a large mixing bowl. Stir to combine well.
4. Transfer the fregola to the mixture and fold it well. Season to taste and serve at room temperature.

Prosciutto Crudo & Leek Involtini

Meaning: Raw Ham & Leek Rolls

Region of Origin: Emilia-Romagna

Wine Pairing: Riesling, Moscato, Chenin Blanc, Rosé, Grenache, and Zinfandel

Time: 35 minutes

Serving Size: 4 portions

Prep Time: 10 minutes

Cooking Time: 25 minutes

Ingredients:

- ∉ 2 medium leeks
- ∉ 5 oz milk
- ∉ 2 tablespoons extra-virgin olive oil
- ∉ 2 tablespoons of flour
- ∉ 12 slices Prosciutto Crudo
- ∉ ¼ cup parmesan, grated
- ∉ ⅔ chives, chopped
- ∉ 1 tablespoon butter
- ∉ Nutmeg, sea salt, and pepper to taste

Directions:

1. Remove the outer parts of the leek. Chop the leek into 3/4 rounds. Wash with a saline solution. Drain the water on a plate lined with a kitchen towel.
2. In a large skillet, heat the olive oil. Fry the leeks until fragrant (5 minutes). The ideal is to continually stir the leeks until they have formed soft ribbons.
3. Remove the leeks from the stove, season with salt and pepper. Allow to cool in the pan.
4. Make a bechamel sauce by combining the butter and flour in a non-stick pan on low heat. Stir continuously until a paste has formed. Add the milk and increase the heat to a medium setting. Stir until it has thickened.
5. Add a pinch of nutmeg and sea salt to taste. Continue stirring until the sauce has thickened some more. Remove from the heat, and allow to cool completely.
6. Stir the leeks and parmesan into the mixture. Prepare the prosciutto slices by adding them to a pan, leaving some space in between them.
7. Add a spoonful of the mixture onto each slice of prosciutto. Sprinkle chives on top, and roll into an involtini.
8. Once all the involtini are rolled, arrange them on plates

or platters in a creative shape.

Chapter 2:
Pasta Dishes

After pizza, pasta is the next dish that embodies the essence of Italian cuisine. Pasta is the kryptonite of many people across the globe. Nearly every country in the world has taken the classic Italian dish and put their own unique spin on it.

Pasta is known as the noodles of the Italian people and is made from durum wheat. Durum wheat is low in moisture and high in gluten, making it a perfect pairing to pasta production. The grain is pressed into sheets, cut into a variety of shapes, and packaged.

Characteristics of Quality, Authentic Pasta

A quality pasta can be recognized as having the following distinguishing features:

- ∉ With the right thickness, the pasta will cook evenly in a short amount of time.

- ∉ It retains its shape, and if cooked al dente, it will remain that way and not become soggy.
- ∉ No starchy outer film will be present after it has been cooked.
- ∉ Cooking water will be clear after the pasta has been cooked. Meaning all nutrients will be retained in the pasta.
- ∉ If made from good quality gluten, the pasta will have an elastic consistency while being eaten.
- ∉ Good quality pasta is porous.
- ∉ The color will be bright yellow before and after the cooking process.

Types of Italian Pasta

There are many different types of pasta in terms of shapes. Each is unique to one of the 2o regions in Italy:

Bigoli - *Veneto*

Chitarra - *Abruzzo*

Gigli - *Tuscany*

Penne - *Campania*

Strozzapreti - *Emilia-Romagna*

Trofie - *Liguria*

Other pasta types include:

Filled pasta

Agnolotti, cappelletti, ravioli, tortellini

Long and skinny shapes

Bucatini, capellini, fusilli lunghi, linguine, spaghetti, spaghettini, vermicelli

Long ribbon-like pasta

Fettuccine, mafaldine, pappardelle, stringozzi, tagliatelle, trenette

Miniature pasta shapes

Anelli, canestrini, fregola, orzo, quadrettini, risi, stelline

Shell shaped

Conchiglie, lumache, lumaconi

Tubular

Cannelloni, ditalini, macaroni, manicotti, penne, rigatoni, paccheri, trenne, tortiglioni

Twisted

Casarecce, fusilli, gemelli, rotini, strozzapreti, trofie.

Why You Should Invest in an Italian Pasta Maker

Investing in a pasta maker will elevate your Italian dishes to another level. Nothing comes close to making your own dough and then lovingly running it through the machine until perfection has been achieved.

There are a significant number of benefits when making use of a pasta machine:

- Send healthy food to your family dinner table because you are aware of the quality and nutrient value of what you made.
- Save time and get more things done in the kitchen when you have a quality pasta maker.
- Have full control over the ingredients and portions you cook and serve with.
- Discourage overeating and being overweight.
- Get the same results as an original Italian restaurant, with pasta dishes of the same quality, every time.
- Create and explore with many great pasta dishes.

Some Renowned Pasta Makers

There are many different brands of Italian Pasta Makers that can be purchased. Each brand has its own unique design, offering, and features. Some of these brands include:

1. CucinaPro Pasta Maker Deluxe
2. Imperia Pasta Maker Machine
3. Marcato Design Atlas 150 Pasta Machine
4. Norpro 1049R Pasta Machine

5. Phillips Kitchen Appliances Noodle Pasta Maker Plus
6. Weston 6 Inch Traditional Style Pasta Machine

Basic Italian Pasta Dough Recipe

Time: 1 hour, 30 minutes

Serving Size: 2 portions

Prep Time: 45 minutes

Cooking Time: 45 minutes

Ingredients:

- 1 ⅔ cups 00 flour
- 2 large eggs
- Sea salt to taste
- 1 tablespoon olive oil

Directions:

1. Clean a surface on the counter with a wet, disinfected cloth. Allow to dry.
2. Sift the flour onto the surface, make a hole in the middle. Add the remainder of the ingredients into the hole.
3. Using the fingers of one hand, gradually work in the flour until a dough has formed. Knead the dough until it has a smooth consistency (2-5 minutes). Cover the ball of dough in plastic wrap. Leave to rest for 30 minutes at room temperature.

4. Follow the instructions on the pasta maker to roll it through the machine.

Pasta Recipes for You to Try at Home

Cjalsons (Cjarsons)

Meaning: Sweet & Savoury Dumplings

Region of Origin: Friulli-Venezia Giulia

Wine Pairing: Grand Pinot Nero

Time: 1 hour, 21 minutes

Serving Size: 2 portions

Prep Time: 1 hour 15 minutes

Cooking Time: 6 minutes

Ingredients:

- ½ cup all-purpose flour
- ½ cup whole wheat flour
- 3 tablespoons butter, melted
- 1 tablespoon butter reserved
- 3 tablespoons water
- 1 egg yolk
- 2 oz minced pancetta
- ½ apple, cubed

- ∉   1 pear, cubed
- ∉   10 crumbled amaretti biscuits
- ∉   Sugar to taste
- ∉   Pepper to taste
- ∉   Salt to taste
- ∉   Cinnamon to taste
- ∉   Parmesan to taste

Directions:

1. In a large bowl, combine the flour, melted butter, and egg yolk. Mix well.
2. Transfer to a clean, lightly flour-dusted surface and knead until the dough becomes soft. Place in a sealable food storage bag, and refrigerate for 30 minutes.
3. Using a medium-sized frying pan, fry the pancetta on medium heat. Add the apple and pear to the pan once the pancetta changes color. Cook until the pear has just turned soft.
4. Add sugar, salt, and pepper to taste. Remove the pan from the heat, and add the crumbled amaretti to the pan. Transfer to a plate.
5. Remove dough from the fridge and roll out on a lightly floured surface until thin. A pasta machine can be used to the same effect as an alternative. Cut the dough into 3.5 mm rounds.
6. Add a teaspoon of filling to the middle of each round, brush water on the outside of the round, and fold it in half. The folded rounds should resemble a half-moon (crescent) shape. Press the edged sealing it.
7. Bring a pot of salted water to a boil on the stove. Melt the remaining butter in a separate skillet on low heat.
8. Divide the cjalsons in batches and cook them in the boiling water. Once they come to the surface, remove

them from the water with a slotted spoon, and transfer them to the pan of butter.

9. Cook for 2-3 minutes, turning them gently. Sprinkle it with parmesan, pepper, and cinnamon.

Pasta alla Norma

Region of Origin: Sicily

Wine Pairing: Nero d'Avola

Time: 1 hour, 10 minutes

Serving Size: 4 portions

Prep Time: 20 minutes

Cooking Time: 50 minutes

Ingredients:

- 2 cups marinara sauce
- 2 medium eggplants, washed
- ¼ cup virgin olive oil + 1 teaspoon set aside for later
- ¼ teaspoon fine sea salt
- 8 oz spaghetti
- ½ cup fresh basil, washed and shredded
- Extra shredded basil for garnish
- 1 teaspoon chili flakes
- ½ teaspoon dried oregano
- ¾ cup parmesan cheese
- 2 large baking sheets, lined with parchment paper

Directions:

1. Preheat the oven to 425°F.
2. Wash the eggplants. Using a peeler, shave ribbons of eggplant off alternating between the skin and flesh. In the end, you will have alternating pieces of white and black ribbons.
3. Discard either end of the eggplant and cut the remainder into rounds. Place the circles on the baking sheets. Brush both sides of the rounds with olive oil. Sprinkle with fine salt.
4. Place the baking sheets in the oven and roast until golden brown on both sides. Remove from the oven and keep aside to cool.
5. Bring a pot of water to a boil, add salt and the pasta. Cook *al dente*. Drain all the water, except for ½ cup. Then return the pasta to the water.
6. In another pot, warm the marinara sauce and stir the eggplant into the sauce. Add the remainder of the olive oil, chili flakes, oregano (crush with your fingers first), and fresh basil.
7. Add the pasta and ½ pasta water to the eggplant and sauce, stir well. Add ⅔ of the cheese and keep the rest aside—season with salt and pepper to taste.
8. Transfer to bowls, garnish and serve.

Anelli alla Pecoraro

Meaning: Pecorara Rings

Region of Origin: Abruzzo

Wine Pairing: Montepulciano

Time: 75 minutes

Serving Size: 8 - 10 portions

Prep Time: 25 minutes

Cooking Time: 50 minutes

Pasta Ingredients:

- 4 cups all-purpose flour
- 1 teaspoon sea salt
- 4 extra-large eggs
- 2 tablespoons olive oil
- ¼ cup lukewarm water
- Avocado oil for frying
- 2 small eggplants cut into thin rounds
- 3 small summer squash cut into rounds
- 3 red bell peppers, finely diced
- A batch of Ragù all'Abruzzese (recipe below), heated to a simmer
- 1 cup ricotta
- Freshly grated parmesan

Ragù all'Abruzzese Ingredients:

- 5 tablespoons olive oil
- 8 oz beef, without the bone - quartered
- 6 oz pork shoulder, without the bone - cut into 3 parts
- 6 oz lamb shoulder, without the bone - cut into 3 parts
- Fine sea salt to taste
- Fresh ground pepper to taste
- 3 lbs canned tomatoes, drained

∉   1 finely chopped red onion

Ragù all'Abruzzese Directions:

1. Warm the avocado oil in a large pot over medium heat. Season the meat and add to the pot. Brown on both sides for 4 minutes. Ensure that the meat is seared all over. Remove from the heat and set aside.
2. Add the tomatoes to a blender and gently blitz.
3. Return the pot to the stove and add the olive oil. Fry the onions until they become fragrant (5 minutes). Pour in the tomatoes and stir well. Bring it to a simmer.
4. Add the meat back into the pot, reduce heat to low. Cover partially with a lid and allow the sauce to simmer. Stir frequently and allow the sauce to cook for 3 hours. The meat should be tender and juicy, and the sauce should be thickened. Adjust the seasoning if desired.
5. Turn the heat off. Remove the meat from the sauce and store for later.

Pasta Directions:

1. Sift and combine the salt and flour in a food processor. Gently drizzle the olive oil in increments. Break the eggs into the mixture. Beat on a low speed.
2. Add the water in sections, and only until the dough has made miniature curds.
3. Lightly dust a work surface with additional flour and transfer the dough to the surface. Knead the dough for several minutes before wrapping it in plastic and allowing it to rest at room temperature for 30 minutes.
4. Cover the work surface with a large, clean cloth. Dust the cloth with flour. Pinch a piece of the dough, the same size as a walnut, and roll it into a rope of ⅛ inches

in diameter. (Keep a bowl of water handy and wet your palms slightly to aid the rolling process.)

5. Cut the rope into 3 ½ inch lengths. Join the ends of the lengths to form a circle. Place the finished ring on the flour-dusted cloth. Continue and repeat the process until all the dough has been rolled and placed on the cloth. (If you are serving the anelli the same day, allow the rings to rest on the cloth for a few hours.)

6. Bring a large pot of salted water to a boil. Add ¼ of avocado oil to a large skillet and heat the oil on medium heat. Add the eggplant and gently fry on both sides for 4 minutes.

7. Transfer the pieces to a waiting plate lined with paper towels, and drain the oil. Fry the summer squash until golden brown and also transfer to the paper towel. Next, fry the peppers until fragrant, and also move to the plate of paper towels containing the other vegetables.

8. Move all the vegetables, with the exception of 1 cup, to the ragù. Gently stir the mixture. Once the water is boiling in the pot, work the anelli in batches to the pot.

9. Cook the anelli *al dente*. Drain all the water except for 1 cup. Return the pasta to the pot and coat with two-thirds of the sauce.

10. Dish and serve with parmesan and ricotta on top.

Bucatini all'amatriciana

Region of Origin: Lazio

Wine Pairing: Sangiovese

Time: 25 minutes

Serving Size: 8 - 10 portions

Prep Time: 5 minutes

Cooking Time: 20 minutes

Ingredients:

- 235 oz peeled Italian tomatoes (canned & drained)
- ¼ cup extra-virgin olive oil
- 1 tablespoon extra-virgin olive oil (additional)
- 1 large red onion, finely chopped
- 2 small chilies, finely chopped and stemmed
- 6 oz pancetta, thinly sliced
- 2 ½ lbs bucatini pasta
- ½ cup pecorino cheese
- 2 tablespoons additional pecorino cheese
- Fine sea salt to taste

Directions:

1. Crush the tomatoes with your hands over a large bowl. Heat the olive oil in a large frying pan. Add the onion and chilies to the pan, and cook for 5 minutes, until fragrant.
2. Next, add the pancetta and cook for 10 minutes. Add the crushed tomatoes and juiced to the pan and reduce it to low heat. Cook for 40 minutes, occasionally stirring until the sauce has thickened. Season with salt.
3. Bring the pasta to a boil in a large pot with salted water—cook the pasta *al dente*. Drain the water and return the pasta to the pot after draining it with a strainer.

4. Add the pecorino and sauce to the pasta in the pot and coat well.

Spaghetti alla Marchigiana

Region of Origin: Marche

Wine Pairing: Zinfandel

Time: 20 minutes

Serving Size: 4 servings

Prep Time: 10 minutes

Cooking Time: 10 minutes

Ingredients:

- 14 oz spaghetti
- 6 oz guanciale, cubed
- 7 oz olive oil
- 1 medium red onion, coarsely chopped
- 1 garlic clove, chopped
- 1 fresh chili pepper
- 8 oz pecorino cheese
- Seasoning to taste
- Dried oregano to taste

Directions:

1. Place the spaghetti in a large pot with salted water and cook *al dente*. In a medium skillet, fry the guanciale, onion, and chili in olive oil on low heat.

2. When the guanciale is crisped, add the onion and the garlic and continue to fry. Add seasoning to taste.
3. Remove the pan from the heat and set aside. Plate the spaghetti into bowls and sprinkle some pecorino on top. Pour the onion mixture on top, mix well and serve.
4. Finish off with some pecorino and freshly ground pepper to taste.

Agnolotti del Plin

Region of Origin: Piedmont

Wine Pairing: Ruché

Time: 2 hours

Serving Size: 6 servings

Prep Time: 20 minutes

Cooking Time: 10 minutes

Pasta Ingredients:

- 400g 00 flour
- 4 eggs

Filling Ingredients:

- 14 oz beef brisket, diced
- 1 oz all-purpose flour
- 1 medium red onion, coarsely chopped
- 2 tablespoons olive oil
- 6 oz dry red wine

- ½ cabbage, chopped roughly
- 2 oz grated Grana Padano
- Fine sea salt and ground pepper to taste

Sauce Ingredients:

- 4 oz unsalted butter
- grated Grana Padano

Directions:

1. Starting with the filling, coat the beef with flour, and shake off excess. Heat 1 oz oil in a large frying pan and brown the meat, searing it on all sides. Add the onion and wine to the pan.
2. Reduce the heat, and allow the alcohol to evaporate, cover the meat with boiling water and cook for 1 hour until tender and juicy. Adjust seasoning and remove from the heat.
3. Place a large pot on the stove and bring salted water to a boil. Add the cabbage to the water and braise for a few minutes. Drain through a strainer and allow to cool.
4. Remove the meat from the liquid and chop finely with the cooled cabbage. Add the grated cheese and season according to taste.
5. Mix until well combined, cover with cling wrap and allow to rest.
6. Moving on to the pasta dough, sift the flour on a clean, dry surface and make a hole in the middle. Crack the eggs into the hole and mix bits of flour in at a time using the fingers of one hand.
7. Knead the dough into a smooth ball with an elastic consistency. Press it flat into a disc shape. Wrap it in cling wrap and allow to rest for 30 minutes at room temperature.

8. Divide the pasta into three equal parts and roll out on a lightly floured surface or through a pasta machine. Trim into long rectangular shapes.

9. Spoon the mixture into the bottom half of each of the 3 rectangles. Fold the sheet over to cover the filling, allowing for ½ inch between. Fold the pasta into small rectangles, sealing the edges by pressing down.

10. Bring a large pot of water to a boil, with added salt. In a medium skillet, melt the butter over medium heat.

11. Cook the plin (pasta) in the boiling water until they float to the surface. Drain on a paper towel and transfer to the pan of melted butter. Turn frequently until they are well coated on both sides in the butter.

    12. Dust with Grana Padano and serve immediately.

Chapter 3:
Meat, Poultry, and Salumi

There are various types of meat, poultry, and salumi or cured meats in Italy, and these can even be looked at granularly in detailed subcategories:

Beef

The four most popular beef producing regions in Italy are Piedmont, Umbria, Marche, Abruzzo, Molise, Emilia-Romagna, Campania, Lazio, and Tuscany.

They are responsible for breeding cattle from which the meat can yield 22 different cuts to be used in classic Italian cooking.

Bresaola

A dry-cured meat from the Lombardy region. Cut from the fillet and can be purchased aged.

Veal

Veal is cows that are less than a year old. It has a very delicate taste in comparison to other beef cuts and also lighter in color.

Poultry

Chicken

Both hens and roosters are used in Italian cooking, with the hens being more common. Chickens are classified by age:

1. Broiler (Pollastro) is 3 to 4 months old and weighs between 21 to 28 oz.
2. Pollo di Grano is 6 months old and weighs 2 lbs.
3. Roaster (Pollo/Pollastra) is about 16 weeks old and weighs between 2 to 2.5 lbs.
4. Capon (Galetto) is male and about 6 months old.
5. Gallo is a male which is two years old and is tough to eat.
6. Gallina is a female, which is old and is only suitable for its

fat and making soup.

Duck

Both wild and domesticated species are used for cooking purposes. Duck meat pairs well with flavors such as tangerine, onions, prunes, cherries, olives, and red wine.

Goose

Goose is predominantly consumed during the Italian festive seasons. The meat is dark in color and goose liver is also used to create pâtés.

Pork

Guanciale

Also known as pork cheeks. It is aged for a minimum period of three months. The triangular shape is similar in texture to that of pancetta, except for the pepper-coated exterior.

Lardo

This is a type of hardened fat that is located in the neck region of the pig. It has a beautiful, delicate aroma.

Pancetta

Also commonly known as *streaky bacon* in American terms. It is made from the belly of the pig and is characterized by layers of alternating meat and fat.

Pork

Mostly used for making all the dry-cured cold cuts such as *salumi* and sausages. Both domestic as well as wild boar can be eaten.

Prosciutto

This cured meat is made from the hind legs of pigs, boars, deer, goats, buffalo, and turkey. It can be consumed *crudo* (raw) on its own or enjoyed on a platter with other cold cuts.

Salumi

It is recommended to instead invest in whole *salumi* as opposed to individual slices. Get the most out of this dish by slicing it at home and consuming it within the span of a few days.

Sausage

Sausages can be made from any of the meat that is produced in Italy. Each region has its own unique spin on the type of sausage it produces.

Lamb

Lamb is a popular choice of meat right through the year in certain regions of Italy. Mutton is a very uncommon occurrence in Italy. There are four types of lamb in this country, and they are *abbacchio* (baby lamb), *agnello* (spring lamb), *agnellone* (lamb), *pecora* (mutton).

Venison/Game

Wild boar can be wild or semi-wild, and a species known as

meticcio, which is a culmination of breeding a domestic pig with a wild boar, is prevalent in commercial swine production.

Moreish Meat, Poultry, and Salumi Recipes

Goulash Triestino

Region of Origin: Friuli-Venezia Giulia

Time: 80 minutes

Serving Size: 6 - 10 servings

Prep Time: 20 minutes

Cooking Time: 60 minutes

Ingredients:

- ⅓ cup avocado oil
- 2 large red onions, cut into quarters
- 2 teaspoons kosher salt
- 2 lbs beef round steak cut into cubes
- 2 teaspoons smoked paprika
- 1 teaspoon oregano (dried)
- 1 twig of fresh rosemary
- 3 cups cold water
- 1 tablespoon 00 flour

- ∉ 4 tablespoons pasta di pomodoro
- ∉ Dollop of sour cream

Directions:

1. Starting with a large skillet, heat the avocado oil. Add the onions and toss in the oil, cooking until fragrant and soft on medium heat.
2. Spread out the onion evenly on the bottom of the pan. Add the cubed beef on top of the onions in one layer. Add salt, rosemary, and paprika. Cover the pan and allow the meat to stew without stirring. Check occasionally to see that the sauce and meat are not burning.
3. After half an hour, cover the pan only partially, lower the heat and stir up the onions and beef. Continue this process for another 30 minutes.
4. Combine the water and flour into the pan. Whisk until the mixture is lump-free and add the tomato paste. Frequently stir the mixture, gently folding the tomato-flour paste into the meat and onions.
5. Cook for 45 minutes to 1 hour. The meat should be tender and the sauce slightly thickened. Adjust seasoning if desired. Allow to stand for a few hours.
6. Reheat the mixture on low heat, adding a little water if required. Serve warm with a dollop of sour cream.

Smacafam

Meaning: Crush-hungry

Region of Origin: Trentino-Alto Adige

Wine Pairing: Rotari Brut

Time: 70 minutes

Serving Size: 8 servings

Prep Time: 30 minutes

Cooking Time: 40 minutes

Smacafam Ingredients:

- 2 tablespoons extra-virgin olive oil
- 1 oz lardo
- 1 red onion, thinly sliced
- 2 garlic cloves, diced
- 4 Italian pork sausages, coarsely rounded
- 6 oz portobello mushrooms, diced
- 1 cup red wine
- 7 oz canned tomatoes
- 1 sprig fresh rosemary

Polenta Ingredients:

- 3 cups chicken stock
- 6 oz polenta
- 1 oz unsalted butter, cubed
- Parmesan cheese, grated (to taste)
- 2 cups of water

Directions:

1. Combine the stock and water in a large pot to boil on medium heat. Add the polenta and stir continuously. Add seasoning and simmer, stirring frequently for 30 minutes. Stir in the butter and 1 oz of the parmesan.

Turn the heat on the lowest setting to keep the polenta warm.

2. Heat the oil and the lardo in a large skillet. Stir every so often until the lardo has been rendered. Add the onion and garlic and cook until fragrant. Add the sausage, brown by stirring frequently.

3. Next, add the wine and the portobello until the liquid has been reduced to half the volume. Combine the tomato and rosemary into the mixture and simmer for 5 minutes.

Lasagna Valdostana

Region of Origin: Aosta Valley

Wine Pairing: Sangiovese

Time: 50 minutes

Serving Size: 4 servings

Prep Time: 5 minutes

Cooking Time: 45 minutes

Ingredients:

- 11 oz lasagna sheets
- 11 oz fontina cheese, cubed
- 7 oz pancetta, diced
- 5 oz parmesan cheese, finely grated
- ½ white wine
- Salted butter at room temperature

- ∉ 1 tablespoon powdered nutmeg
- ∉ 2 cups milk
- ∉ Sea salt and ground pepper to taste

Directions:

1. Preheat the oven to 356°F.
2. Combine some butter and the pancetta in a skillet. Add half of the wine and reduce the heat until half of the liquid has evaporated. Remove from the heat and set aside.
3. In another non-stick pan, add the cheese, milk, nutmeg, and salt and cook on medium heat. Stir frequently until the cheese has melted.
4. Prepare an oven dish by adding a generous layer of cooking spray along the bottom and sides. Spoon some fontina sauce at the bottom. Add a layer of lasagna.
5. Next, add tablespoons of fondue and cooked ham and spread evenly with the back of a wooden spoon. Sprinkle grated parmesan and freshly ground pepper. Repeat the process until all the ingredients have been used.
6. Bake in the oven for 30 minutes. Turn off the heat and keep the dish inside the oven for another 5 minutes. Serve and enjoy!

Saltimbocca

Meaning: Jumps in the mouth

Region of Origin: Lazio

Wine Pairing: Malbec, Cabernet Sauvignon

Time: 50 minutes

Serving Size: 4 servings

Prep Time: 5 minutes

Cooking Time: 45 minutes

Ingredients:

- 4x veal fillets, each weighing +/- 3 ounces
- 8 slices prosciutto
- 16 marjoram leaves
- 2 oz unsalted butter
- ½ cup red wine
- Fine sea salt and black pepper to taste
- Olive oil

Directions:

1. Using 2 sheets of parchment paper, place each fillet in the middle thereof. Roll each of them out to 5 mm thickness. Season with salt and pepper.
2. Add 2 marjoram leaves and 2 slices of prosciutto to the top of each fillet. Fold in the edges.
3. Heat 1 teaspoon of olive oil in a large skillet. Sauté each fillet on all sides for 2 minutes. Remove the fillets from the pan and place on a cutting board to rest for a few minutes.
4. Heat the unsalted butter in the same pan as the fillets until the butter is browned. Add the wine and whisk until emulsified.
5. Divide the fillets into 4 serving dishes and dress with the butter sauce.

Pampanella Molisana

Meaning: Spicy roast pork from Molise

Region of Origin: Molise

Wine Pairing: Sparkling Glera Prosecco

Time: 50 minutes

Serving Size: 4-6 servings

Prep Time: 5 minutes

Cooking Time: 45 minutes

Ingredients:

- 3 lbs mixed pork cuts
- Sea salt, powdered garlic, and white wine vinegar to taste
- 5 tablespoons chili flakes or powder
- 5 tablespoons sweet, unsmoked paprika

Directions:

1. Ask your butcher to make ¾ inch slices to the bone of the pork cuts. Place the meat snugly together in an oven-proof dish of 9 inches in diameter.
2. Prepare the chili and paprika rub by combining them and adjusting the spice level as desired.
3. Sprinkle the meat with sea salt and the powdered garlic. All the meat should be covered, but not overly so.
4. Repeat the same process with the chili-paprika rub.

Ensure all areas, both inside and out, are covered with the rub. Marinate in the fridge for at least 3 hours or overnight.

5. Preheat the oven to 350°F. Measure a piece of parchment paper that has the circumference of covering the meat in the dish completely.

6. Wet the parchment paper slightly and wring out excess water. Cover the meat with the wet parchment paper and tuck the sides in to seal the dish. Cover the dish with tin foil and bake in the oven for 1 hour 50 minutes.

7. Remove from the oven, drizzle lightly with white wine vinegar. Cover and return to the oven for 10 minutes.

Chapter 4:
Italian Fish Cuisine

Feast of the Seven Fishes

The exact origin of this tradition is a bone of contention. It comprises a sit-down dinner table feast where a total of seven fish dishes are consumed. Tradition dictates that it has to be seven different types of fish, prepared seven different ways.

It appears that this culinary observance is more popular amongst Americans, and very few Italians have adopted this part of their heritage. This practice is typically done every Christmas Eve. The number seven is believed to be connected to numerous Catholic symbols.

In the bible, the number seven is repeated more than 700 times. According to the Roman Catholic Church, the seven courses of the feast are linked to the seven days of Creation and the seven deadly sins as shown in (*The Origin of the Feast of the Seven Fishes*, 2019)

If you are a family of pescatarian food lovers and you would like to try your hand at this feast, I can recommend the following dishes for you to try (in sequential order):

1. *Acciughe Marinate alla Ligure* (Marinated Anchovies)
2. *Brodetto di Branzino* (Wild Sea Bass Soup)
3. *Crudo di Pesce* (Fish Tartare)
4. *Paccheri con Sugo di Mare* (Seafood Pasta)
5. *Pesce al Forno* (Baked Fish)
6. *Pesce alla Griglia* (Grilled Fish)
7. *Pesce in Umido* (Fish with Roasted Fennel and Taggiasca Olives)

Fregola allo Scoglio

Region of Origin: Sardinia

Wine Pairing: Combinate Vermentino

Time: 45 minutes

Serving Size: 4 servings

Prep Time: 20 minutes

Cooking Time: 25 minutes

Ingredients:

- 1 teaspoon saffron
- ¼ dry white wine
- 2 tablespoons extra-virgin olive oil
- ½ lb shrimp, deveined and shelled
- ½ lb scallops
- 1 small red onion, finely chopped
- 2 minced garlic cloves
- 2 cups chicken stock
- 1 cup fregola
- ½ clams, scrubbed
- 2 tablespoons freshly minced parsley
- Sea salt and freshly ground pepper to taste

Directions:

1. In a pestle and mortar, crush the saffron, add the wine, and put aside for later.
2. Add the olive oil to a large, cast-iron pot and heat over high heat. Add the shrimp and sear for 1 minute on each side. Place the seared shrimp in a separate bowl. Add the scallops and repeat the process. Move to the same bowl containing the shrimp.
3. Pour the remaining oil, garlic, and onion into the pot. Cook until fragrant. Reduce to medium heat and season with salt and pepper as desired.
4. Combine the clams into the pot, and cover with the lid—steam for 3 minutes. Add the shrimp and scallops to the pot. Cook for 3 more minutes.
5. Spoon the mixture into 4 waiting bowls, sprinkle with parsley and serve.

Brodetto alla Vastese

Meaning: Spicy roast pork from Molise

Region of Origin: Abruzzo

Wine Pairing: Trebbiano d'Abruzzo

Time: 1 hour, 20 minutes

Serving Size: 4 servings

Prep Time: 20 minutes

Cooking Time: 1 hour

Ingredients:

- 3.5 lbs fish
- 4 cloves garlic
- A few slices of bread
- 8 cuttlefish
- ½ cup extra-virgin olive oil
- ¼ cup of red onion
- Fine sea salt to taste
- 8 medium-sized shrimp (deveined and shelled)
- 2 cups tomato purée
- 1 tablespoon fresh parsley
- 1 large chili pepper
- 1 oz muscles
- 1 oz clams

Directions:

1. Heat the olive oil in a large skillet over medium heat. Combine the tomato and garlic and cook until fragrant. Add the tomato and parsley. Bring to a boil for 5 minutes.
2. Pour 2 cups of boiling water into the skillet, add the cuttlefish and boil for 10 minutes.
3. Add the other seafood to the pan at a gradual pace. Continue cooking for another 10 minutes. If the juices are too thick, then dilute with some warm water.
4. Fry the slices of bread in a pan with some olive oil until crisp. Dip the bread into the seafood dish and sauce.

Risotto alla Pescatora

Region of Origin: Campania

Drink Pairing: Bicchiere di vino bianco

Time: 46 minutes

Serving Size: 4 servings

Prep Time: 20 minutes

Cooking Time: 26 minutes

Ingredients:

- 14 oz Arborio rice
- 1.1 lb mixed seafood
- 3 oz olive oil
- 1 garlic clove
- 1 medium-sized mild chili

- 2 tablespoons tomato paste
- 3 ½ oz white wine
- 4 cups fish stock
- ½ teaspoon fresh black pepper
- Sea salt to taste
- Parsley to taste

Directions:

1. If you are using frozen fish, defrost, open the packet and dry with kitchen towels.
2. Heat the olive oil in a large pan over low heat. Add the garlic, onion, and the chili and cook until fragrant.
3. As soon as the garlic is golden, remove it from the pan and discard it. Remove the chili from the pan and discard it.
4. Turn the heat to medium and add the seafood to the pan. Combine well with the oil, and cook for just 3 minutes.
5. Remove the seafood with a slotted spoon and place it aside in a bowl. Cover the bowl with tinfoil.
6. Add the rice to the pan and coat well. Stir for 2 minutes. Add the wine and keep stirring until it evaporates.
7. Add the stock in spoonfuls to the pan and reduce to low heat. During this process, keep stirring gently at a continuous pace.
8. When half of the stock is added, pour in the tomato paste. Stir until an orange-colored sauce is achieved. Adjust the salt and pepper seasoning if required.
9. Add the seafood to the pan, stirring frequently until the rice is *al dente*. Add the parsley and stir.

Lumache alla Bresciana

Region of Origin: Lombardy

Drink Pairing: Montonale La Venga

Time: 3 hours

Serving Size: 4 servings

Prep Time: 2 hours

Cooking Time: 60 minutes

Ingredients:

- 7 oz snail/escargot meat
- 1 finely chopped red onion
- 1 tablespoon tomato paste
- 14 oz roughly shredded spinach
- ¼ cup olive oil
- ⅔ oz salted butter
- 1 tablespoon dried parsley
- ⅔ grated parmesan
- 1 carrot, peeled and rounded
- 2 cloves garlic
- 2 spring onions, finely chopped
- 1 medium celery stalk coarsely rounded
- Fine sea salt and pepper to taste

Directions:

1. Bring a large pot of salted water to a boil. Add the snail meat. Simmer for 10 minutes and scoop off any residue

that might rise to the surface. Remove from the pot with a slotted spoon, shaking off excess water.

2. Place the meat in a bowl and cover with white wine vinegar. Marinade for 3 hours. Rinse under running water and set aside.

3. Add the carrot, spring onion, and celery to a pan of cold water together with the snail meat and white wine.

4. Bring the liquid to a boil, and simmer for 1 hour. Separate the meat from the rest of the pan, place in a bowl, and cover with a clean dishcloth.

5. In a large saucepan, melt the butter and oil together. Place all of the spinach in the pot. Add the onion and garlic and cook until fragrant.

6. Add the meat and cook for another 3 minutes. Next, add the tomato paste and stir well.

7. Combine the spinach with the rest of the ingredients in the pot. Cook covered for 20 minutes on low heat. Adjust seasoning if required.

8. Stir in the parsley and cook for 20 minutes.

Bagna cauda

Meaning: *hot bath*

Region of Origin: Piedmont

Wine Pairing: Nebbiolo

Time: 20 minutes

Serving Size: 6 servings

Prep Time: 5 minutes

Cooking Time: 15 minutes

Ingredients:

- ¾ cup extra-virgin olive oil
- 6 tablespoons salted butter at room temperature
- 12 fillets of anchovy
- Mixed choice vegetables cut into small cubes
- 1 lb Italian bread, cut into sections of 2 inches

Directions:

1. Combine the butter, anchovies, and oil into a food processor and blend well. Transfer the mixture to a medium-sized skillet.
2. Cook on a low heat for 15 minutes, stirring on occasion. Season with salt and pepper.
3. Transfer mixture to a fondue pot over heat. Serve with bread and fresh vegetables.

Whitebait With Dill Mayonnaise

Region of Origin: Liguria

Wine Pairing: Muscadet, Picpoul

Time: 30 minutes

Serving Size: 1 serving

Prep Time: 10 minutes

Cooking Time: 20 minutes

Ingredients:

- 2 tablespoons cumin seeds
- 2 tablespoons mayonnaise
- 1 cup extra-virgin olive oil
- 2 oz 00 flour
- 16 oz whitebait
- 1 lime
- Fresh dill chopped
- Fish spice, sea salt, and freshly ground pepper to taste

Directions:

1. Heat the olive oil in a large skillet over a medium heat.
2. In a large mixing bowl, sift the flour. Crush the cumin seeds and add this to the sifted flour. Season to taste with the spices.
3. Portion the whitebait in batches. Coat in the flour and fry in the oil until crispy and golden brown. Remove from the pan and drain on a plate with kitchen towels.
4. Combine the dill and the mayonnaise and add freshly squeezed lime to taste. Put the mayo dip in the middle of a platter, add the whitebait and serve.

Chapter 5:
Rice Dishes for the Win

Italy is a rice-producing country that yields approximately 1.3 million tons of rice annually. The majority of this product is then shipped out to its neighboring countries on the European continent.

Rice production predominately comes from the Lombard, Piedmont, and Veneto regions. These regions have been grain producers since the 15th century.

The Italians boast modern and sustainable techniques that are aimed at preserving the country's resources.

Rice Is Born in Water and Must Die in Wine

Risotto ai Mirtilli e Speck

Region of Origin: Trentino-Alto Adige

Wine Pairing: Dogajolo Bianco

Time: 20 minutes

Serving Size: 1 serving

Prep Time: 5 minutes

Cooking Time: 15 minutes

Ingredients:

- 13 oz carnaroli rice
- 7 oz blueberries
- 3.5 oz speck, cut into strips
- 4 cups vegetable stock
- 1 oz unsalted butter
- 1 oz grated parmesan cheese
- 1 small red onion
- Fresh rosemary
- ½ glass of red wine
- Olive oil
- Salt and pepper to taste

Directions:

1. Heat a knob of butter and the blueberries in a large skillet. Fry for a few minutes, and then cover with a lid and cook until soft. Transfer to a blender and combine on high speed until a purée-like consistency has been achieved. Put the purée aside for now.
2. In another pan, heat a few teaspoons of oil. Chop the onion, cook until fragrant and then brown the speck. Stir the mixture occasionally.
3. Add the rice and toast it for 3 minutes. Increase the heat to a high setting. Add the red wine and allow the liquid to evaporate. Lower the heat and add ladles full of stock at a time while the risotto is cooking.
4. When the risotto is halfway done, add the blueberry purée to the pan. Stir frequently. If more moisture is needed, keep adding spoons full of the stock.
5. When the risotto is done, remove the pan from the heat, add the grated cheese, rosemary, and remaining butter. Stir well.
6. Let the mixture rest for a few minutes. Serve topped with blueberries.

Italian Wild Rice Soup

Region of Origin: Emilia-Romagna

Time: 8 hours, 25 minutes

Serving Size: 8 servings

Prep Time: 25 minutes

Cooking Time: 8 hours

Ingredients:

- 1 lb pork meat
- 4 cups of warm water
- Extra-virgin olive oil
- 3.5 oz beef broth or stock
- 1 can diced tomatoes
- 6 oz tomato paste
- 1 large red onion, chopped
- ¾ cup uncooked wild rice, drained and rinsed
- 6 cloves minced garlic
- 2 tablespoons mixed herbs
- ½ teaspoon smoked paprika
- 1 teaspoon cumin seeds
- ¼ crushed chili flakes
- 19 oz shredded baby spinach
- ½ cup grated parmesan cheese
- Sea salt, pepper to taste

Directions:

1. Heat some olive oil in a large pan and add the pork. Cook until the color is no longer pink and break up the chunks of meat with a spoon. Sear on all sides.
2. Add the seared pork, water, broth, tomatoes, tomato paste, rice, garlic, mixed herbs, paprika, cumin, and seasoning to a slow cooker.
3. Cook on a low setting for 7 hours or on a high heat setting for 4 hours. Stir the spinach into the soup until well combined. Serve with grated parmesan on top.

Piedmontese Carnaroli Risotto With Veal Tongue, Hazelnuts, and Grana Padano

Region of Origin: Piedmont

Time: 70 minutes

Serving Size: 8 servings

Prep Time: 10 minutes

Cooking Time: 60 minutes

Veal Tongue Ingredients:

- 1 tongue of veal
- 1 chopped carrot (peeled)
- 1 chopped celery stalk
- 1 finely chopped red onion
- 1 bay leaf
- 2 whole black peppercorns
- 1 oz Piedmontese hazelnuts

Risotto Ingredients:

- 6.5 cups vegetable broth
- 8 oz carnaroli rice
- 2 oz unsalted butter
- 3 oz grated Grana Padano
- Olive oil
- Fine sea salt
- Freshly ground black pepper

Directions:

1. Preheat the oven to 356°F.
2. Add the tongue and all the ingredients to prepare it in a large pot. Cover everything with water and bring to a boil. Reduce the heat and cook on a simmer for 2 hours. Remove from the heat and allow to cool in the liquid.
3. After the veal has rested for 3 hours, strain through a sieve into another pan. Reduce on the stove to low heat, until the liquid is a dark, rich color.
4. Remove the tongue from the liquid, and peel with a paring knife. Place in the fridge to rest for 45 minutes.
5. Place the nuts in a food processor and grind into a powder, set aside for later.
6. Next up is the risotto. Using a large skillet, pour the stock into the pan, and heat over a medium setting.
7. Add a dash of olive oil and toast the rice for 2 minutes, stirring frequently.
8. Season the risotto to taste. Add the stock, spoonfuls at a time. Before adding the next spoonful, allow the risotto to absorb the last round of liquid first. Stir continuously for 20 minutes, until the risotto is creamy.
9. Cut a 7 oz portion of veal into cubes. Season to taste with salt and pepper and brown in a small frying pan with a bit of olive oil.
10. As soon as the risotto is cooked, remove the pan from the heat and stir in the cheese.

Risotto Primavera

Region of Origin: Veneto

Time: 25 minutes

Serving Size: 6-8 servings

Prep Time: 15 minutes

Cooking Time: 10 minutes

Ingredients:

- 1 medium-sized carrot, peeled
- 4 tablespoons extra-virgin olive oil
- 8 ounces asparagus spears
- 1 medium zucchini seeded and trimmed
- 1 medium-sized summer squash quartered
- 4 ½ cups chicken stock
- 1 finely chopped red onion (large)
- 1 ¾ cup Arborio rice
- ¾ cup dry white wine
- 4 medium-sized carrots - peeled
- 4 oz grated parmesan
- 1 cup peas
- ¼ cup of salted butter
- ½ cup basil leaves
- ¼ cup cashew nuts
- Additional grated parmesan

Directions:

1. Cut the medium-sized carrot into strips. Heat 1 tablespoon of olive oil over medium-high heat. Add the asparagus spears, zucchini, and summer squash. Sprinkle it with salt and pepper.
2. Bring the stock to a simmer in a medium skillet over low heat. Cover and keep warm as far as possible.
3. Heat 3 tablespoons of olive oil in a large pot over medium heat. Add the onion and the 4 carrots and cook until fragrant. Add the rice and cook *al dente*. Add the

wine and cook for 3 minutes. Add 1 cup of stock and carrots, simmer for 4 minutes and add 2 more cups. Cook for 10 minutes.

4. Combine the fried vegetables and 1 cup of stock. Simmer for 5 minutes.

5. Add 1 1/3 cups of the cheese, peas, butter, and another 1/2 cup broth. Simmer the mixture until the butter has melted and the rice, and veggies are tender. The risotto should be creamy. Add the basil and season with salt and pepper.

Chapter 6:
Vegetarian Dishes

One of the key characteristics of Italian cooking is the approach of having only a few fresh ingredients on hand to concoct dishes that are packed with flavor.

Some of the key vegetables that are prevalent in classic Italian cooking are (but not limited to):

- Artichokes
- Asparagus
- Aubergine
- Beans
- Beetroot
- Bell peppers
- Broccoli
- Carrots
- Cauliflower

- Celery
- Corn
- Fennel
- Greens
- Mushrooms
- Onions
- Peas
- Potatoes
- Summer squash
- Tomatoes
- Winter squash

Wholesome Vegetarian Recipes

Fave e Cicoria

Meaning: Fava bean purée with wild chicory

Region of Origin: Puglia

Time: 65 minutes

Serving Size: 4 servings

Prep Time: 5 minutes

Cooking Time: 60 minutes

Ingredients:

- 7 oz fava beans, split

- 1 bay leaf
- 1 clove garlic, crushed
- Vegetable broth
- 3.5 oz chicory
- Avocado oil
- Salt and pepper to taste

Directions:

1. In a large skillet, combine the beans, bay leaf, garlic clove, and salt. Cover with vegetable broth.
2. Simmer for 60 minutes until the beans are slushy (add more stock in spoonfuls at a time to avoid burning).
3. When a purée has formed, remove the bay leaf and the garlic clove from the mixture. Season according to taste. Add a dash of olive oil.
4. Wither the greens in a little olive oil in another skillet with a pinch of salt and a tablespoon of water.
5. Plate the purée with a dollop of wilted greens.

Erbazzone

Meaning: Swiss-chard pie

Region of Origin: Emilia-Romagna

Time: 70 minutes

Serving Size: 4 servings

Prep Time: 10 minutes

Cooking Time: 60 minutes

Dough Ingredients:

- ∉ 2 cups all-purpose flour
- ∉ Fine sea salt to taste
- ∉ Good quality olive oil
- ∉ Water

Filling Ingredients:

- ∉ 2.2 lbs swiss-chard, washed and shredded
- ∉ 3.5 oz pancetta or prosciutto
- ∉ 3 tablespoons avocado oil
- ∉ 1 red onion, coarsely diced
- ∉ 3.5 oz grated parmesan
- ∉ Salt and pepper to taste

Directions:

1. Sift the flour and salt in a large mixing bowl. Add the oil and ¾ of water. Knead into an elastic ball of dough. Place the dough in a resealable bag and refrigerate for 1 hour.

2. Chop the beetroot and blanch the stems in hot water. Drain of moisture and put aside. Heat some olive oil in a large pan on medium heat. Add the pancetta or prosciutto and cook until the fat has been rendered. Stir in the onion and cook until fragrant.

3. Combine the spinach, beet leaves, and stems. Toss in the fat. Cover the pan and allow it to cook. When the greens have withered, remove the lid and cook until the liquid has dissipated. Remove from the heat and allow to cool.

4. Preheat the oven to 392°F. Line the baking sheet with parchment paper.

5. Divide the dough into 2 equal parts. Roll out the first

half as thin as possible to cover the surface of the baking sheet. Arrange on the lined baking sheet.

6. Fold the cheese into the spinach and spread the filling evenly on top of the dough. Repeat the same process with the second ball of dough and arrange this on top of the filling.
7. Fold and seal the dough's edges and brush with egg wash or a little bit of oil.
8. Bake for 30 minutes or until golden brown and crisp.

Frittata Rafano e Pecorino

Meaning: Horseradish and pecorino dish

Region of Origin: Basilicata

Time: 45 minutes

Serving Size: 6 servings

Prep Time: 10 minutes

Cooking Time: 35 minutes

Ingredients:

- 11 oz mashed spunta potatoes
- 8 free-range chicken eggs
- 3 oz grated pecorino cheese
- 1 oz horseradish
- Extra-virgin olive oil
- Sea salt and pepper to taste

Directions:

1. Preheat the oven grill section to 392°F.
2. The mash needs to be cooled down, but still warm enough, and not cook the eggs.
3. In a large skillet, heat some olive oil on medium heat. Crack the eggs into the pan and add the mashed potato. Next, add the pecorino and horseradish, seasoning to taste.
4. Cook together for 5 minutes until it becomes fragrant. Remove the pan and place it under the grill for a few minutes.

Parmigiana Stacks

Meaning: Eggplant stacks

Wine Pairing: Casascarpa

Time: 15 minutes

Serving Size: 4 servings

Prep Time: 5 minutes

Cooking Time: 10 minutes

Ingredients:

- ½ batch of marinara sauce
- 13 oz ricotta cheese
- 1 free-range chicken egg
- Garlic powder, salt, pepper to taste
- 1 cup fresh oregano

- ¼ cup grated parmesan
- 1 large eggplant
- 2 tablespoons of olive oil
- Mozzarella cheese

Directions:

1. Preheat the oven to 375°F. Prepare a large baking sheet with parchment paper.
2. Slice the eggplant into an equal number of rounds with a thickness of 1 inch each. Rub both sides (including the edges) with oil and spices. Place the rounds on the baking sheet.
3. Bake on both sides for 15 minutes, until just tender but golden in color. Remove from the oven and remove from the sheet.
4. Line the baking sheet with a fresh layer of parchment paper. Place the 4 largest rounds down first. Spread a layer of ricotta and a generous slice of mozzarella on each. Add a tablespoon of marinara sauce to each portion of eggplant. Continue the process creating 4 stacks. Save some marinara sauce for serving.
5. Return to the oven and bake for 10 minutes. Serve with marinara sauce and sprinkle parmesan on top.

Chapter 7:
Italian Bread

Italian bread is soft and light, fluffy on the inside and crisp on the outside. There are 17 types of bread that are popular amongst its patrons:

1. Tartalli
2. Piadina
3. Penia
4. Panettone
5. Pane di Altamura *DOP*
6. Pane Casareccio di Genzano *IGP*
7. Pane Carasau
8. Pandoro
9. Grissini
10. Fragguno
11. Focaccia

12. Farro della Garfagnana *IGP*
13. Faranita
14. Coppia Ferrarese *IGP*
15. Colomba Pasquale
16. Ciabatta
17. Cecìna

Italian Bread Recipes

Ligurian Focaccia

Time: 65 minutes

Serving Size: 1 flatbread

Prep Time: 5 minutes

Cooking Time: 60 minutes

Dough Ingredients:

- 1 ½ cups of tepid water
- ½ teaspoon active dry yeast
- 2 ½ teaspoons honey
- 5 ⅓ cups oo flour
- 1 tablespoon of sea salt
- Olive oil
- Rosemary twigs
- Flaked sea salt

Brine Ingredients:

- 1 ½ teaspoons fine sea salt
- ⅓ cup tepid water

Directions:

1. Combine the water, honey, and yeast in a mixing bowl and stir until dissolved. Sift the flour and salt into a large mixing bowl and add the yeast mixture and oil. Cover and rest at room temperature for 12 hours. It needs to grow double in size.
2. Add 3 tablespoons of olive oil to a baking sheet and coat well by turning until the whole surface is covered. Pour the dough out into the baking sheet. Pour 2 tablespoons of oil on top of the dough and spread throughout.
3. Stretch the dough for 30 minutes until the bottom is completely covered and spread evenly. Press dimples in the dough with your first 3 fingers at an angle, repeat a few times.
4. Make the brine by stirring the ingredients thereof together until the salt is dissolved. Pour over the dimples until covered. Leave to rise for 45 minutes. Preheat the oven to 450°F.
5. Sprinkle the focaccia dough with the flaky sea salt and arrange the rosemary stalks. Bake for 30 minutes. Then turn the oven to grill and crisp for 7 minutes.
6. Remove from the oven and brush with olive oil. Allow to rest for 5 minutes. Remove from the pan and serve.

Gnocchi di Pane Raffermo

Meaning: Italian Bread Dumplings

Time: 25 minutes

Serving Size: 4 servings

Prep Time: 20 minutes

Cooking Time: 5 minutes

Gnocchi Ingredients:

- 6.5 oz stale white bread
- 5 oz sultanas or raisins
- 5 oz grated parmesan
- 1 cup 00 flour
- 2 free-range chicken eggs
- 1 teaspoon ground cinnamon
- Nutmeg, sea salt to taste
- Milk

Dressing Ingredients:

- 2 oz salted butter, melted
- 2 marjoram leaves

Directions:

1. Combine the bread and milk in a large bowl and allow to rest for 15 minutes. The bread needs to be soft.
2. Soak the raisins in a separate bowl with tepid water for 5 minutes. Squash the bread with your hands, removing any excess milk.
3. In a large mixing bowl, add the bread, parmesan, nutmeg, salt, raisins, eggs, and flour. Mix with a spoon until well combined.
4. Using a large pot with plenty of salt, bring it to a boil. Add tablespoons of the mixture to the water. When the dumplings start to float on the top, remove them with

a spoon, and transfer to a warm plate.

5. Warm the butter and marjoram leaves in a pan. Pour the dressing over the dumplings and sprinkle parmesan on top.

Homemade Veneto Ciabatta Bread

Time: 1 hour, 55 minutes

Serving Size: 1 loaf

Prep Time: 10 minutes

Rising Time: 1 hour, 30 minutes

Cooking Time: 25 minutes

Ingredients:

- 1 cup and 1 tablespoon of water, divided
- ½ teaspoon honey
- 2 teaspoons active dry yeast
- 2 cups and 3 tablespoons of 00 flour, divided
- 1 teaspoon fine sea salt

Directions:

1. Combine ¼ cup water, honey, and yeast in a bowl and allow to rest for 5 minutes before stirring. Sift the flour in a large mixing bowl. Make a hole in the center, and add the yeast mixture and water in the well. Mix well and when almost done, add the salt. Sprinkle the top of the dough with 1 ½ tablespoon of flour.

2. Cover the bowl with a tea towel and allow to rest for 1

hour 30 minutes.

3. Preheat the oven to 425°F. Prepare a baking sheet by lining it with parchment paper. Transfer the dough ball to the baking sheet, careful to keep the flour on top intact.

4. Using a spoon, form the dough into a log shape. In the bottom tray of the oven, place a tray with 6 ice cubes in the middle. Bake the dough for 25 minutes.

Crescia Sfogliata

Meaning: Flaky flatbread

Region of Origin: Le-Marche

Time: 45 minutes

Serving Size: 1 loaf

Prep Time: 20 minutes

Cooking Time: 25 minutes

Ingredients:

- 18 oz all-purpose flour
- 1 free-range egg
- 3 oz lard + additional 2 oz for layers
- 3 oz lukewarm milk
- 4 oz water
- 1 heaped teaspoon fine sea salt
- Freshly ground black pepper to taste

Directions:

1. Sift the flour in salt into a large mixing bowl. Add the milk, egg, and water. Mix to form a dough. Allow the dough to sit uncovered for 20 minutes. Place dough on a lightly floured surface.
2. Pull on one side of the dough and fold it into the middle. Repeat the process with the opposite side.
3. Turn the dough 90 degrees and repeat the previous step. Roll the dough over and leave to rest for 20 minutes.
4. Divide the dough into portions of 5 oz each. Pull one side of each portion to the middle section. Pull the opposite side and join them in the middle.
5. Turn the dough 90 degrees and repeat the previous step. Roll the dough over and leave to rest for 20 minutes.
6. Using a spray bottle, lightly spritz the surface with olive oil. Roll out each portion to a thickness of 2 mm.
7. Brush the flat tops with lard, dividing it into equal parts. Roll each portion up to form a tube.
8. Roll the ends inwards to each other. Heat a pancake pan to a medium heat and add a bit of olive oil.
9. Respray the working surface again with more oil and roll the dough out to a 3mm thickness.
10. Fry each flatbread for 2 minutes a side.
11. Place one crescia on a plate, add your choice of toppings. Place another crescia on top and cut into slices to serve.

Tuscan Panzanella Salad

Region of Origin: Tuscany

Time: 35 minutes

Serving Size: 6 servings

Prep Time: 10 minutes

Cooking Time: 25 minutes

Ingredients:

- 2 ½ lbs tomatoes, cubed
- 2 teaspoons fine sea salt + additional for later
- ¾ sourdough bread, cut into cubes of 1 ½ inches in diameter
- 10 tablespoons olive oil, divided
- 2 tablespoons of diced red onion
- 2 teaspoons crushed garlic
- ½ teaspoon hot mustard
- 2 tablespoons white wine vinegar
- Black pepper to taste
- ½ oz fresh basil leaves

Directions:

1. Place the tomatoes in a strainer over the sink and season with 2 teaspoons sea salt. Shake to coat well. Drain for a total of 15 minutes, tossing regularly.
2. Preheat the oven to 350°F. Combine the bread and 2 tablespoons of oil in a large mixing bowl. Shake the bread to coat it in the oil. Apply a generous layer of cooking spray to a large cookie sheet.
3. Move the bread to the baking sheet and bake in the oven for 15 minutes. Remove and allow to cool. Add the tomatoes, garlic, onion, mustard, and vinegar to a mixing bowl. Whisk well. Add the remainder of the olive oil to the mixture. Adjust seasoning as desired.

4. Add the toasted bread and basil to the mixture. Shake gently to coat. Allow the mixture to rest for half an hour before serving.

Chapter 8: Desserts

This is the chapter that most people probably looked forward to. There are many different dessert and pastry recipes; it was almost impossible to add just a few favorites for you to make and enjoy at home!

Delicious Italian Desserts

Pressnitz

Meaning: *"Walnut crescents"*

Region of Origin: Friuli-Venezia Giulia

Time: 60 minutes

Serving Size: 6 servings

Prep Time: 20 minutes

Cooking Time: 40 minutes

Ingredients:

- 2.5 oz sultanas
- 2.5 oz raisins
- ½ cup rum
- 5 oz walnuts
- 5 oz almonds
- 1 oz pine nuts
- 3.5 oz dark chocolate
- 3.5 oz breadcrumbs
- 5 oz granulated sugar
- ½ teaspoon cinnamon
- 3 oz candied peel
- 1 lemon zest, grated
- 1 orange zest, grated
- 2 free-range eggs
- 3 oz salted butter, melted
- 10 oz puff pastry
- Egg wash made from 1 egg yolk

Directions:

1. Soak the raisins and sultanas in the rum for 1 hour. Drain the liquid and set aside. Store the raisins and sultans for later.
2. Preheat the oven to 356°F. Combine the nuts and chocolate in a food processor, gently blitz together.
3. Pour the nuts and chocolate into a large mixing bowl.

Add the raisins, sultanas, breadcrumbs, sugar, cinnamon, zests, candied peel, and stir well.

4. Beat the eggs with a fork in a small mixing bowl and add them to the mixture. Next, add a bit of rum and the melted butter. Gently stir until a paste has formed.

5. Roll out the pastry into a rectangle of 50x20 cm. Trim the edges, so they are of equal size.

6. Spoon the mixture on one side of the dough and roll up to form a sausage. Brush a little egg yolk on the edge to make it stick to the dough. Close the ends by folding the pastry under, creating a spiral-like shape.

7. Brush with egg yolk and bake for 40 minutes.

Cannoli Siciliani

Region of Origin: Sicily

Time: 1 hour, 50 minutes

Serving Size: 24 portions

Prep Time: 1 hour, 30 minutes

Cooking Time: 20 minutes

Cannoli shell ingredients:

- 2 cups 00 flour
- 1 free-range egg
- 1 tablespoon olive oil
- 1 tablespoon brown sugar
- ¼ cup red wine
- 3 tablespoons full fat milk

- 1 egg white, separated
- Olive oil for frying

Ricotta filling ingredients:

- 4 cups of ricotta
- ¾ cup icing sugar
- Pinch of cinnamon
- ½ cup of dark chocolate chips
- 1 cup finely chopped pistachios
- Additional powdered sugar for dusting on top.

Directions for the shells:

- Sift the flour in a large bowl, and make a depression in the middle. Pour in the egg, wine, sugar, and milk. Gently stir the ingredients in the middle, combining bits of flour each time. Knead into a dough ball.
- Divide the dough ball into a few equal portions. Roll them out on a lightly floured surface to ⅛ mm thickness. Cover with a clean, dry kitchen towel.
- Cut rounds of 4 inches in diameter. Repeat with all the dough. Wrap the dough pieces around a bamboo dowel or a cannoli mold. Seal the edges with the beaten egg white.
- Add the oil to a large pot, filling it halfway and then heating it. Fry the cannoli shells until golden brown. Remove from the oil and allow to drain on a plate with kitchen towel.

Directions for the filling:

1. Combine all of the ingredients in a mixing bowl until smooth. Transfer to a piping bag and pipe the mixture into the shells, equally dividing it.
2. Dip the ends of the cannoli in pistachio and chocolate

chips. Dust with icing sugar.

Torta con le Mele

Meaning: Apple cake

Region of Origin: Trentino-Alto Adige

Time: 1 hour, 50 minutes

Serving Size: 24 portions

Prep Time: 1 hour, 30 minutes

Cooking Time: 20 minutes

Ingredients:

- 1 cup unsalted butter at room temperature.
- 1 ½ cup all-purpose flour, plus additional for dusting
- 1 tablespoon baking powder
- 1 teaspoon fine sea salt
- ¾ cup brown sugar
- 3 eggs
- ¼ Grappa
- 3 green apples, peeled and cored (1 apple to be thinly sliced, 2 apples coarsely chopped)

Directions for the filling:

1. Preheat the oven 350°F. Grease an 8-inch springform tin with the butter and dust lightly with flour. Shake off excess flour.
2. Sift the flour, salt, and baking powder into a medium

mixing bowl. Using an electric mixer, beat the sugar and butter until creamy. Add the eggs and Grappa, beat again.

3. Pour into the flour mixture and combine well. Stir in the 2 chopped apples.

4. Pour the mixture into the springform tin. Sprinkle the remaining apple on top. Bake for 40 minutes. Remove from the oven, and place on a cooling rack for another 15 minutes.

5. Remove from the tin, place on a platter. Dust with icing sugar, cinnamon and serve with cream, ice cream, or evaporated milk.

Pasticioto

Region of Origin: Puglia

Time: 56 minutes

Serving Size: 12 pastries

Prep Time: 30 minutes

Cooking Time: 26 minutes

Dough Ingredients:

- 1 3/4 cups all-purpose flour
- Dash of sea salt
- ½ cup brown sugar
- 1 teaspoon baking powder
- 1 free-range egg at room temperature
- 1 free-range egg yolk at room temperature

- ½ cup salted butter at room temperature + 2 tablespoons extra for later

Custard Ingredients:

- ¾ cup full fat milk
- ¾ heavy whipping cream
- 4 egg yolks
- ½ cup brown sugar
- ½ teaspoon vanilla essence
- 2 ½ tablespoons all-purpose flour
- 2 medium lemon peels

Directions for the custard:

1. Heat the milk, lemon peels, and cream over a low heat in a medium pot. Remove from the heat and allow to cool.
2. Combine the yolks and sugar in another medium-sized pot. Add the vanilla and the flour and whisk well. Remove from the heat and strain the liquid, discarding the lemon peel. Whisk until the custard is thick and lump-free. Move to a bowl and cover with cling wrap; refrigerate for 1 hour.

Directions for the dough:

1. Sift all the dry ingredients into a large mixing bowl. Combine the rest of the ingredients into another mixing bowl and beat well.
2. Make a well in the middle of the dry ingredients and combine bits of flour at a time. Once the dough has formed, roll out on a lightly floured surface until soft.
3. Wrap the dough in cling wrap and refrigerate for half an hour. Preheat the oven to 350°F.
4. Prepare the rolling surface by lightly dusting a bit more

flour. Knead the dough ball a few times until it's soft. Roll out to 8 mm thickness and cut in circles of 3 ½ inches.

5. Spray a muffin or cupcake tin with a generous layer of cooking spray. And place a dough circle at the bottom. Using a toothpick, poke a few holes at the bottom. Fill the individual tins with the custard.

6. Wet your finger slightly in cold water and run along the rim of each tin. Place another dough circle on top, and firmly but gently seal with your fingers.

7. Brush the top with egg wash and bake in the oven for 40 minutes. Remove from the oven and allow to cool. Dust with icing sugar.

Tartufo

Region of Origin: Calabria

Time: 55 minutes

Serving Size: 4 servings

Prep Time: 15 minutes

Cooking Time: 10 minutes

Salted Caramel Sauce Ingredients:

- ½ cup brown sugar
- ¼ cup water
- ⅓ cup double cream
- 1 teaspoon vanilla extract
- ½ teaspoon flaked sea salt

Tartufo Ingredients:

- 1 cup crushed Oreo cookies
- ½ cup dark chocolate, chopped
- 1-pint vanilla gelato
- 4 maraschino cherries
- 4 twigs of fresh mint

Directions for the salted caramel:

1. In a large saucepan, add the sugar and water, and cook on a medium heat setting until golden brown.
2. Remove from the heat and stir in the remaining ingredients. Allow to cool to room temperature.

Directions for the tartufo:

1. Add the crumbled cookies and chocolate into a sealable plastic bag.
2. Using an ice cream scoop, scoop a ball of gelato into the spoon. Poke a hole in the middle and insert 1 cherry. Cover the hole and gently drop the ball into the bag to cover it with the cookies and chocolate. Place on a tray when done.
3. Repeat the process with the other 3 balls. Freeze for at least 30 minutes.
4. Serve by halving the tartufo and spooning the warm salted caramel on top. Garnish with mint.

Caragnoli

Region of Origin: Molise

Time: 1 hour, 5 minutes

Serving Size: 24 servings

Prep Time: 45 minutes

Cooking Time: 20 minutes

Ingredients:

- 3 free-range eggs at room temperature
- 3 tablespoons brown sugar
- 3 tablespoons canola oil
- 2 cups all-purpose flour
- ¼ teaspoon baking powder
- 1 ½ cup of honey
- 3 cups peanut oil

Directions:

1. In a medium mixing bowl, crack the eggs and beat until frothy. Add the sugar and whisk again. Add the canola oil and whisk well.
2. Combine the flour and dough and sift bits of baking powder into the mixture. Add the dry ingredients to the wet ingredients. Knead the dough for 5 minutes. Cover the bowl with plastic wrap and allow it to rest for half an hour.
3. Cut the dough into 4 equal parts. Roll out in an elongated shape of ⅛ inch in thickness. Form them into the desired shape. Heat the peanut oil and fry each piece of dough for 30 seconds on a side.
4. Remove the pastry from the oil and place on a tray to drain on the kitchen towel. Heat the honey and drizzle the pastries. Serve immediately.

Conclusion

There are many interesting facts and stories that relate to Italian food and the customs that accompany them.

The 10 top-rated Italian food customs are:

Mealtimes. Italians are very punctual when it comes to the times that they eat their food. Lunch is typically served at one o'clock in the afternoon, and dinner is served at eight o'clock.

Order of events. Traditionally the formal Italian sit-down meal consists of five courses. The sequence is:

1. Antipasto
2. Primo
3. Secondo
4. Contorno
5. Dolce

Lots of dishes to wash. Not everything you see in a movie is real. But in this case, it is. There are always mountains of dirty dishes that need to be washed after every meal. This is because it is a tradition to eat each meal on its own plate.

Salad sides. Salads are served as accompanying dishes, and only a tourist will order this as a dish on its own. Don't feel offended if your request is not adhered to, though.

Cheese and fruit. Each meal is ended with fruit and cheese unique to the region the meal is consumed in.

Coffee. Coffee is nearly close to a religion in Italy and is consumed daily at intervals and anytime in between.

Milk consumption. Milky drinks or consuming milk on its own is reserved for breakfast times only and will be frowned upon otherwise.

Drinks during meals. Wine, mineral water, beer, and soda (kids) are on the list of approved drinks during mealtimes.

Seafood does not get any cheese. No authentic Italian dish will have any form of cheese in it. The fish species all present a delicate palate and will be ruined by the pungent nose of cheese.

***Soffritto* - the staple.** The base ingredient in most classic Italian dishes is called *soffrito*. It can be made by combining onion, celery, and carrots that have all been diced finely and frying them in olive oil until fragrant (5 minutes).

Italian Cooking A Glossary of Terms

Disclaimer: Glossary of terms stated below is a derivative of https://memoriediangelina.com/glossary/**

Arrosto: Meaning any food that is roasted.

Arrosto Morto: Any food that is cooked by roasting it in a pan. This is a term used to describe a method that combines both wet and dry cooking.

All'agro: A green or other ingredient that is cooked briefly then drizzled with olive oil and lemon juice. The lemon juice is also sometimes substituted with vinegar, but less often.

Alla brace: It means to grill.

Al dente: This is the nirvana of pasta when it is perfectly cooked.

It should have a firm but elastic texture in your mouth.

Al forno: This means a dish that is cooked in the oven.

Alla griglia: This refers to meat, vegetables, and anything in between that has been barbecued.

Al vapore: Means a dish that is steamed.

Aromi: A collective noun used to describe fragrant herbs such as ginger and garlic.

Antipasto: Translated to English, it means "before the meal" and is referring to the hors d'oeuvre.

Battuto: Refers to vegetables that are finely chopped.

Bianco or in bianco: Bianco or in bianco means white. This can be a pasta or pizza dish that is only made with cheese. Or a lasagne drenched in bechamel sauce.

Bollito: Means boiled when translated into English.

Condimento: Means a dish whereby one ingredient is used as a buddy to flavor another.

Contorno: A dish made of vegetables that is served with the third course of a traditional meal (secondo).

Crema: Refers to a soup created making veggies that were puréed first.

Cucina povera: Refers to a dish that was made from ingredients from a region that is considered to be poor and having little money.

Fare la scarpetta: Means to sop up the sauce and juices in your plate, using slices of bread to mop it up.

Fritto: Referred to as frying a dish. This can be poultry, meat, fish, or even vegetables.

Gnocchi: The Italian word for dumpling.

In umido: A dish that is served with an accompanying tomato-based sauce.

In brodo: Translated, this means "in broth." It is one of the ways to serve pasta, which is a contrast to "dry" pasta.

In padella: Means to fry leafy green vegetables.

Insaporire: An important Italian cooking term, meaning to fry in a base sauce called a sofrito.

In zimino: A term that describes a Tuscan cooking method where the seafood is cooked with leafy greens.

Mantecare: This term refers to whisking, beating, etc. when a sauce or a dish needs to have a smooth, creamy texture.

Minestra: The generic Italian word for soup.

Minestrone: A literal translation meaning "big soup." This is usually a soup that comprises a lot of ingredients that yields into a thick soup.

Odori: This refers to the veggies and herbs that are combined in a *battuto*.

Pasta asciutta: Means a dry pasta that is dressed with sauce.

Pasta all'uovo: Means a fresh egg pasta.

Pasta fresca: Fresh homemade pasta from Italy's Northern region.

Peperoncino: A little red hot chili pepper. It is predominantly used when cooking dishes from Southern Italy.

Primo piatto or primo: Means the first course of a daily Italian mealtime.

Piatto unico: a Meal that is served either during the first or second courses of a meal.

Quanto basta, or q.b: Its literal translation means "more or less."

Ragù: Means a tomato-based sauce that simmers for a prolonged period of time.

Rosolare: Means to lightly fry in oil or butter.

Secondo piatto or secondo: Refers to course number two during a formal sit-down feast.

Spaghettata: A meal that was spontaneously and made unplanned with pasta.

Spianatoia: The wooden surface on which fresh pasta is prepared.

Stuzzichini: Refers to eats or snacks at an event to nibble on.

Sugo: This is a tomato-based pasta sauce.

Trifolati: Means to fry mushrooms.

Un filo d'olio: Means a steady stream of olive oil being poured into a dish.

Vellutata: A soup that has a creamy texture and is made from vegetables.

Zuppa: Means a rustic Italian soup.

Italian Folk Sayings Translated

Chi se move mangia e chi sta fermo secca.

He who moves eats, he who stands still, dries up.

Mangiare per vivere e non vivere per mangiare.

Eat to live and not live to eat.

A tavola non si invecchia.

At the table with good friends and family, you do not become old.

L'Appetito vien mangiando.

Appetite comes with eating.

Chi va a letto senza cena tutta la notte si dimena.

He who goes to bed without eating will regret it throughout the night.

Il riposo da ristoro—solo dopo un buon lavoro.

The rest from refreshment—only after good work. (Meaning) The pleasure one derives from refreshments is enhanced after one has done a good day's work.

Nessuno conosce che cosa sta cucinando nella vaschetta meglio di chi fa la mescolatura.

No one knows what is cooking in the pan better than the one doing the stirring.

Chi la sera i pasti gli ha fatti, sta a gli altri a lavar i piatti.

If one cooks the meal, then the others wash up.

Troppi cuochi guastano la cucina.

Too many cooks spoil the broth.

Chi la vuole cotta e chi la vuole cruda.

Some want it cooked, and some like it raw. (Equivalent) Different strokes for different folks.

La cucina piccola fal la casa grande.

A small kitchen makes the house significant. (Equivalent) The best things in life are free.

Quando la pera e matura, casca da se.

When the pear is matured, it will fall by itself. (Equivalent) All things happen in their own good time.

Una cassetta di mele e arance.

It doesn't make sense to compare two situations to make a point, as the two cases are entirely different from each other.

I frutti proibiti sono i piu dolci.

Forbidden fruit is sweetest.

Esse nufesso qui dice male di macaroni.

One has to be an idiot to speak ill of macaroni.

Amicizie e maccheroni, sono meglio caldi.

Friendships and macaroni are best when they are warm.

Che mangiamo oggi?

What are we going to eat today?

Pane, pesce fritto e baccala!

Bread, fried fish, and dried cod. (Equivalent) There's nothing much to eat.

Chi dorme non piglia pesci.

The early bird catches the worm.

Non si fanno frittate senza rompere le uova.

You have to take action if you want to bring about change.

E meglio l'uovo oggi di una gallina domani.

A bird in the hand is worth two in the bush.

Camminare sulle uova.

Walking on eggshells.

La gallina vecchia fa buon brodo.

The old hen makes a good broth.

Pan di sudore, miglior sapore.

The bread that comes out of sweat tastes better.

Non si vive di solo pane.

One does not live by bread alone.

A chi trascura il poco manchera pane e fuoco.

Stop and smell the roses. Or, Be grateful for what you have.

Pane al pane, vino al vino.

Bread is bread; wine is wine. (Equivalent) To call a spade a spade.

A chi ha fame e buono ogni pane.

All bread is good when you're hungry.

Il pane apre tutte le bocche.

Bread opens all mouths.

E buono come il pane.

English: (Literally) It's as good as bread.

La fame muta le fave in mandorle.

(Literally) Hunger softens fava beans [and makes them sweet]. Meaning: When you're hungry, you don't care about the quality of the food you're eating

Tutto fumo e niente arrosto.

All smoke and no roast. (Meaning): It's no big deal.

Tanto va la gatta al lardo che ci lascia lo zampino.

The cat goes so often to the lard that she will eventually leave her paw print on it.

Belle parole non pascono i gatti.

The poor don't need speeches; they need food.

O di paglia o di fieno purche il corpo sia pieno.

Something is better than nothing.

Aprile freddolino, molto pane e meno vino.

April is a little cold, with lots of bread and not much wine.

Se maggio e scuro, pane sicuro.

If May is dark, bread for sure. (Meaning) If there is poor weather in May, all there will be to eat is bread and not much else.

Bere acqua la mattina e una buona medicina.

Drinking water in the morning is good medicine.

L'acqua corrente non si corrompe mai.

The best things in life are free.

Perdersi in un bicchier d'acqua.

(Literally) To lose oneself in a glass of water. (Equivalent) To make a mountain out of a molehill.

Tanta va la gatta al lardo che ci lascia lo zampino.

(Literally) The pitcher goes so far from the [water] well that it leaves its handle. (Equivalent) A pitcher that is often used is likely to get broken.

Acqua passata non macina piu.

(Literally) Used water doesn't mill anymore. Or Water that's flowed past the mill grinds no more. (Equivalent) What's done, is done. Or It's no use crying over spilled milk.

Una cena senza vino e come un giorno senza sole.

A meal without wine is like a day without sunshine.

Amici e vini sono meglio vecchie.

Friends and wine are best aged.

L'acqua fa male e il vino fa cantare.

Water hurts, and wine makes you sing.

Riempi il bicchere quando e vuoto, vuota il bicchiere quando e pieno, non lo lasciar mai vuoto, non la lasciar mai pieno.

(Literally) Fill your glass when it is empty, empty it when it is full, never leave it blank, never leave it whole.

Luva cattiva non fa buon vino!

Rotten grapes can't give you good wine.

Botte buona fa buon vino.

A good cask makes good wine.

(Dialect): Dumandig' a l'ost' se el gha del bun' vin. El te dis' si!.

(Literally) Ask the innkeeper if the wine is good. Of course, he'll answer yes. Equivalent: Ask a stupid question, and you'll get a silly answer.

Non domandare all'oste se ha buon vino.

Don't ask the host if he has good wine.

Il vino e buono se l'ostessa e bella.

Wine is good if the landlady is beautiful.

Il bicchiere della staffa.

(Literally) The (wine) glass of the stirrup. (Equivalent) One for the road.

Nel vino la verita.

In wine, the truth.

A marzo taglia e pota, se non vuoi la botte vuota

(Literally) In March, cut and prune if you don't want to get hit with nothing. (Equivalent) In March, cut and prune, or you'll not have a good harvest.

References

4 Most Popular Italian Beefs. (2020, November 15). Www.Tasteatlas.com. https://www.tasteatlas.com/most-popular-beefs-in-italy

Animal husbandry - Italy - import, farming. (n.d.). Www.Nationsencyclopedia.com. https://www.nationsencyclopedia.com/Europe/Italy-ANIMAL-HUSBANDRY.html

Appetit, B. (2004, August 20). *Risotto Primavera*. Epicurious. https://www.epicurious.com/recipes/food/views/risotto-primavera-107905

Avey, T. (2012, July 26). *Uncover the History of Pasta | The History Kitchen | PBS Food*. PBS Food. https://www.pbs.org/food/the-history-kitchen/uncover-the-history-of-pasta/

Bagna Cauda. (2004, August 20). Epicurious. https://www.epicurious.com/recipes/food/views/bagna-cauda-2827

BBC Good Food. (n.d.). *A guide to the pasta shapes of Italy*. BBC Good Food. Retrieved November 14, 2020, from https://www.bbcgoodfood.com/howto/guide/guide-pasta-shapes-italy

Boitano, B. (n.d.). *Tartufo*. Food Network. https://www.foodnetwork.com/recipes/brian-boitano/tartufo-recipe-1918820

Button, J. (2020, June 10). *Italian wine labels: Understanding DOCG, DOC & IGT*. Decanter. https://www.decanter.com/learn/italian-wine-labels-understanding-docg-doc-igt-439719/

Capo. (2017, July 18). *spaghetti alla marchigiana*. Iloveitalianfood. http://www.iloveitalianfood.it/en/spaghetti-alla-marchigiana-en/

Casella, C. (2000, October). *Bucatini all'Amatriciana Recipe*. Food & Wine. https://www.foodandwine.com/recipes/bucatini-allamatriciana

Clark, M. (2019, January 24). *Homemade Pasta Dough*. Leite's Culinaria. https://leitesculinaria.com/40229/recipes-homemade-pasta-dough.html

CookiesandKate. (2020, September 30). *Pasta alla Norma Recipe*. Cookie and Kate. https://cookieandkate.com/pasta-alla-norma-recipe/

Costardi Brothers. (n.d.-a). *Veal Tongue Risotto Recipe - Great Italian Chefs*. Www.Greatitalianchefs.com. https://www.greatitalianchefs.com/recipes/piedmontese-veal-tongue-risotto-recipe

Cottonbro. (2020). None. In *Italian Grandma*. https://www.pexels.com/photo/food-woman-texture-pasta-4057692/

DeLallo. (n.d.). *Italian Tradition: Antipasti | Appetizer or Meal.* DeLallo. https://www.delallo.com/blog/antipasti-meal-social-gathering-or-both/

Eataly. (2019, December 4). *The Origin of the Feast of the Seven Fishes.* Eataly. https://www.eataly.com/us_en/magazine/culture/origin-feast-seven-fishes/

Ehlers, M. (2020). Bread on White Plastic Pack. In *Ciabatta Bread.* https://www.pexels.com/photo/bread-food-wood-breakfast-4198359/

Elda Rita Tessadori. (2013, January 30). *Italian Food Customs and Traditions - Ciao Pittsburgh.* Ciao Pittsburgh. https://www.ciaopittsburgh.com/italian-food-customs-and-traditions/

Essential Italy. (2019a). *10 Interesting Facts About Abruzzo | Essential Italy.* Essential Italy. https://www.essentialitaly.co.uk/blog/10-interesting-facts-abruzzo

Essential Italy. (2019b, January 28). *10 Fun Facts You Didn't Know About Puglia.* Essential Italy. https://www.essentialitaly.co.uk/blog/10-things-didnt-know-puglia

Essential Italy. (2019c, September 30). *10 Fascinating Facts about Umbria.* Essential Italy. https://www.essentialitaly.co.uk/blog/10-fascinating-facts-umbria

Fregola Salad With Olives, Orange Zest & Fresh Herbs. (n.d.). Ginodecampo. https://www.ginodacampo.com/recipe/fregola-salad-olives-orange-zest-fresh-herbs/

Glossary of Italian Cooking Terms. (2017, January 13). Memorie Di Angelina. https://memoriediangelina.com/glossary/

Granoro il Primo. (2012). *Granoro.it - How to recognise good quality pasta.* Granoro.It. https://www.granoro.it/en/c/31/the-world-of-granoro/20/high-quality-production/34/how-to-recognise-good-quality-pasta

greatbritishchefs. (n.d.-a). *Erbazzone Recipe - Great Italian Chefs.* Www.Greatitalianchefs.com. https://www.greatitalianchefs.com/recipes/erbazzone-recipe

greatbritishchefs. (n.d.-b). *Fave e Cicoria Recipe – Fava Bean Purée - Great Italian Chefs.* Www.Greatitalianchefs.com. https://www.greatitalianchefs.com/recipes/fave-e-cicoria-recipe-fava-bean-dip

greatbritishchefs. (n.d.-c). *How to Make Saltimbocca - Great Italian Chefs.* Www.Greatitalianchefs.com. Retrieved November 16, 2020, from https://www.greatitalianchefs.com/how-to-cook/how-to-make-saltimbocca

greatbritishchefs. (n.d.-d). *Parma Ham Parcels Recipe - Great Italian Chefs.* Www.Greatitalianchefs.com. https://www.greatitalianchefs.com/recipes/prosciutto-di-parma-parcels-recipe

greatbritishchefs. (n.d.-e). *Rafanata – Horseradish and Pecorino Frittata Recipe - Great Italian Chefs.* Www.Greatitalianchefs.com. https://www.greatitalianchefs.com/recipes/rafanata-recipe

Gross, T. (2011, March 24). *How "Italian Food" Became A*

Global Sensation | WBUR News. Wbur.org; WBUR. https://www.wbur.org/npr/134628158/how-italian-food-became-a-global-sensation

Guerero, A. (2020). Cannoli with Pistachios. In *Cannoli*. https://www.pexels.com/photo/cannoli-with-pistachios-4078183/

Guerrero, A. (2020). Lasagna on White Ceramic Plate. In *Lasagna*. https://www.pexels.com/photo/lasagna-on-white-ceramic-plate-4079520/

Horizon Content. (n.d.). Cooked Food on White Ceramic Plate. In *Seafood risotto*. https://www.pexels.com/photo/cooked-food-on-white-ceramic-plate-3763826/

Italian Bread Facts and Nutritional Value. (n.d.). Health Benefits Times. Retrieved November 17, 2020, from https://www.healthbenefitstimes.com/italian-bread/

Italian Made. (n.d.). *Protected and Certified Italian Products*. Www.Italianmade.com.Au. https://www.italianmade.com.au/page/italian-products

Italian Notes. (2013, March 6). *Gondola facts - 10 interesting facts about Venetian gondolas*. Italian Notes. https://italiannotes.com/gondola-facts/

Italian Word of the Day: Nonna. (n.d.). ThoughtCo. https://www.thoughtco.com/italian-word-of-the-day-nonna-4039731

Italiaoutdoors. (2016, September 22). *Torta Con Le Mele - Apple Cake from Northern Italy*. Honest Cooking. https://honestcooking.com/torta-con-le-mele-apple-cake-northern-italy/

Italy - Agriculture, forestry, and fishing. (2019). In *Encyclopædia Britannica*.

https://www.britannica.com/place/Italy/Agriculture-forestry-and-fishing

Italy - Finance. (n.d.). Encyclopedia Britannica. https://www.britannica.com/place/Italy/Finance

Italy hunting trips. (n.d.). Www.Bookyourhunt.com. https://www.bookyourhunt.com/en/hunting-in-italy

Jacqui. (2020a, July 5). *Lasagna Valdostana from the Aosta Valley.* The Pasta Project. https://www.the-pasta-project.com/lasagna-valdostana-from-the-aosta-valley/

Kenzi Lopez Alt, J. (2020, April 7). *Classic Panzanella Salad (Tuscan-Style Tomato-and-Bread Salad) Recipe.* Www.Seriouseats.com. https://www.seriouseats.com/recipes/2015/09/classic-panzanella-salad-recipe.html

Kevmrc. (2020b, March 22). *30 Interesting Facts About Sardinia, Italy - [100% true facts].* Kevmrc.com. https://www.kevmrc.com/interesting-facts-about-sardinia-italy

Knowles, E., Featherby, L., & Storey, A. (2012, April 9). *Smacafam.* Gourmet Traveller. https://www.gourmettraveller.com.au/recipes/browse-all/smacafam-11447

Knutson, A. (2019, September 24). *Samin Nosrat's Ligurian Focaccia Is Just as Magical as It Looks.* Kitchn. https://www.thekitchn.com/samin-nosrat-salt-fat-acid-heat-ligurian-focaccia-22949343

Kolt, K. (2019, June 12). *Wines of Southern Italy tend to be ripe, round, and juicy, thanks to the weather.* The Georgia Straight. https://www.straight.com/food/1253841/wines-southern-italy-tend-be-ripe-round-and-juicy-thanks-weather

LauraLee. (2019a, October 1). *Calabria Italy – 10 Fun Facts*. Digging Up Roots in the Boot. https://digginguprootsintheboot.com/calabria-italy-10-fun-facts/

LauraLee. (2019b, November 26). *Campania Italy-10 Fun Facts*. Digging Up Roots In The Boot. https://digginguprootsintheboot.com/campania-italy-10-fun-facts/

LauraLee. (2020c, February 25). *Friuli Venezia Giulia Italy – 10 Fun Facts*. Digging Up Roots in the Boot. https://digginguprootsintheboot.com/friuli-venezia-giulia-italy-10-fun-facts/

LauraLee. (2020d, March 10). *Molise Italy - 10 Fun Facts*. Digging Up Roots in the Boot. https://digginguprootsintheboot.com/molise-italy-10-fun-facts/

LauraLee. (2020e, March 24). *Tuscany Italy - 10 Fun Facts*. Digging Up Roots in the Boot. https://digginguprootsintheboot.com/tuscany-italy-10-fun-facts/

LauraLee. (2020f, July 7). *Marche Italy 10 Fun Facts*. Digging Up Roots in the Boot. https://digginguprootsintheboot.com/marche-italy-10-fun-facts/

LauraLee. (2020g, August 11). *Valle d'Aosta Italy 10 Fun Facts*. Digging Up Roots in the Boot. https://digginguprootsintheboot.com/valle-daosta-italy-10-fun-facts/

LauraLee. (2020h, September 8). *Emilia Romagna Italy 10 Fun Facts*. Digging Up Roots in the Boot. https://digginguprootsintheboot.com/emilia-romagna-italy-10-fun-facts/

LauraLee. (2020i, October 13). *Lombardia Italy 10 Fun*

Facts. Digging Up Roots in the Boot. https://digginguprootsintheboot.com/lombardia-italy-10-fun-facts/

Lazzaris, S. (2019, July 18). *How Rice Is Grown In Italy*. Www.Foodunfolded.com. https://www.foodunfolded.com/how-it-works/rice-the-italian-way

Lisa. (n.d.-b). *cjarsons Archives*. Very EATalian. Retrieved November 15, 2020, from http://www.veryeatalian.com/tag/cjarsons/

Lovegood, L. (2020). Sliced Bread With Sliced Vegetables on Brown Wooden Chopping Board. In *Italian Antipasti*. https://www.pexels.com/photo/sliced-bread-with-sliced-vegetables-on-brown-wooden-chopping-board-4087611/

Maria. (2018a, December 20). *Caragnoli di Maria: A Molisan Christmas Tradition*. She Loves Biscotti. https://www.shelovesbiscotti.com/caragnoli/

Meat, Poultry and Salumi. (2012, May 21). Living a Life in Colour. https://www.livingalifeincolour.com/kitchen/ingredients/meat-poultry-and-salumi/#go-beef

Miquel, J. (2015, February 4). *Italian Wine & Cheese Pairing Part 2*. Social Vignerons. http://socialvignerons.com/2015/02/04/italian-wine-and-cheese-pairing-part-2/

Nadia. (2019, January 12). *Sicilian Cannoli with Ricotta Filling*. Mangia Bedda. https://www.mangiabedda.com/sicilian-cannoli-with-ricotta-filling/

Necchio, V. (n.d.-a). *Peperoni all'Acciuga Recipe - Great Italian Chefs*. Www.Greatitalianchefs.com. https://www.greatitalianchefs.com/recipes/peperoni-all-acciuga-recipe

Necchio, V. (n.d.-b). *Taralli Pugliesi Recipe - Great Italian Chefs*. Www.Greatitalianchefs.com. Retrieved November 14, 2020, from https://www.greatitalianchefs.com/recipes/taralli-pugliesi-recipe

Paola. (2014, March 12). *Gnocchi di Pane Raffermo (Italian Bread Dumplings)*. Passion and Cooking. http://www.passionandcooking.com/2014/03/12/gnocchi-di-pane-stale-bread-dumplings/

Pezzaioli, F. (n.d.-a). *Garden snails Brescia (Lumache alla bresciana)*. Www.Italyum.com. https://www.italyum.com/specials/172-garden-snails-brescia-lumache-alla-bresciana.html

Pezzaioli, F. (n.d.-b). *Seafood risotto (Risotto alla pescatora)*. Www.Italyum.com. https://www.italyum.com/risotto-recipes/183-seafood-risotto8.html

Pixaby. (n.d.). Ribbon Pastry Pasta on Fettuccini. In *Italian Pasta*. https://www.pexels.com/photo/yellow-pasta-spaghetti-eat-42326/

Prestia, T. (2020, August 20). *Pampanella Molisana*. Tinas Table. https://www.tinastable.com/pampanella-molisana/

PRWEB UK. (2017, October 3). *Parma Ham Shares Wine Pairing Ideas*. Benzinga. https://www.benzinga.com/pressreleases/17/10/p10129579/parma-ham-shares-wine-pairing-ideas

Quintanilla, V. (2020, April 19). *Eggplant Parmesan Stacks recipe with wine pairing*. Girl's Gotta Drink. https://girlsgottadrink.com/eggplant-parmesan-stacks-recipe-with-wine-pairing/

Rebecca. (2019, October 4). *13 Great Films set in Sicily to Inspire you to Visit.* Almost Ginger. https://almostginger.com/films-set-in-sicily/

Ricetta Risotto ai mirtilli e speck. (n.d.). Il Cucchiaio d'Argento. https://www.cucchiaio.it/ricetta/ricetta-risotto-mirtilli-speck/

Rosemary. (2018b, November 27). *Easy No Knead Homemade Italian Ciabatta Bread.* An Italian in My Kitchen. https://anitalianinmykitchen.com/homemade-italian-ciabatta-bread/

Rosemary. (2019c, May 13). *Pasticciotti Italian Cream Filled Tarts.* An Italian in My Kitchen. https://anitalianinmykitchen.com/italian-cream-filled-pastry/

roughguides. (n.d.). *Trentino-Alto Adige | Italy Travel Guide | Rough Guides.* Www.Roughguides.com. https://www.roughguides.com/italy/trentino-alto-adige/

Russock, C. (2011, August 23). *Anellini alla Pecorara Recipe | Cook the Book.* Www.Seriouseats.com. https://www.seriouseats.com/recipes/2011/08/anellini-alla-pecorara-recipe.html

Sauced & Found. (n.d.). *Twenty Italian Pantry Staples.* Sauced & Found. Retrieved November 13, 2020, from https://www.saucedandfound.com/blog/2020/5/20/20-italian-pantry-staples

Siano, P. (2014, May 8). *10 Things About Basilicata: It's Not Just a Bunch of Rocks!* Tour Italy Now. https://www.touritalynow.com/blog-basilicata-not-just-a-bunch-of-rocks/

Smyth, D. (2019, March 15). *6 Italian Ham Types | eHow.com.* EHow.com.

https://www.ehow.com/list_7450792_italian-ham-types.html

Sonoma, W. (2017, October 3). *Easy Seafood Fregola Recipe | Williams Sonoma Taste*. Williams-Sonoma Taste. https://blog.williams-sonoma.com/easy-seafood-fregola-recipe/

Taste Atlas. (n.d.). *Abruzzese Food Homepage: Discover Abruzzese Cuisine | TasteAtlas*. Www.Tasteatlas.com. https://www.tasteatlas.com/abruzzo

The Proud Italian. (2020a, August 2). *Your Favorite Italian Antipasti.* The Proud Italian. https://theprouditalian.com/your-favorite-italian-antipasti/

The Proud Italian. (2020b, September 9). *What Are The 5 Regions of Italy?* The Proud Italian. https://theprouditalian.com/what-are-the-5-regions-of-italy/

Vacayholics. (2011, June 18). *Facts About Piedmont.* Vacayholics. https://vacayholics.com/facts-about-piedmont

van Heerden, F. (2017). Assorted Colour Houses Beside Body of Water. In *Italy Boot*.

Velouria. (2007, May 8). *Goulash Triestino Recipe - Food.com.* Www.Food.com. https://www.food.com/recipe/goulash-triestino-244505

Walks of Italy. (2012, June 8). *8 Things to Love About Emilia Romagna, Italy.* Walks of Italy. https://www.walksofitaly.com/blog/things-to-do/why-visit-emilia-romagna-and-bologna-italy

Walks of Italy. (2019, July 9). *The Regions of Italy.* Walks of Italy Blog. https://www.walksofitaly.com/blog/traveltips/italy-by-region

Wei-Duan, W. (2017, June 11). *Crescia sfogliata (flaky flatbread) – Le Marche*. Living a Life in Colour. http://www.livingalifeincolour.com/recipes/crescia-sfogliata-flakey-flatbread-le-marche/

World Strides. (2016, October 20). *WorldStrides*. WorldStrides. https://worldstrides.com/blog/2016/10/12-interesting-facts-about-rome/

Printed in Great Britain
by Amazon